NALBINDING

NALBINDING
It's not knitting!

Heritage techniques for the
contemporary textile crafter

Sally Pointer

Herbert Press

LONDON · OXFORD · NEW YORK · NEW DELHI · SYDNEY

HERBERT PRESS

Bloomsbury Publishing Plc

50 Bedford Square, London, WC1B 3DP, UK

Bloomsbury Publishing Ireland Limited,

29 Earlsfort Terrace, Dublin 2, D02 AY28, Ireland

BLOOMSBURY, HERBERT PRESS and the Herbert Press logo are trademarks of Bloomsbury Publishing Plc

First published in Great Britain 2026

A catalogue record for this book is available from the British Library

Library of Congress Cataloguing-in-Publication data has been applied for

ISBN: PB: 978-1-78994-306-1; eBook: 978-1-78994-308-5

4 6 8 10 9 7 5 3

Typeset in Freight Sans Pro
by JerryGoldieGraphicDesign

Printed and bound in Slovenia by DZS Grafik

To find out more about our authors and books visit www.bloomsbury.com and sign up for our newsletters

For product safety related questions contact productsafety@bloomsbury.com

Page 1 image: Dalby stitch tablet case (see pages 130–6)

Page 2 image: Nalbinding can make timeless basketry as well as softer garments

Page 3 image: A Coptic child's sock in progress (see pages 71–4)

Contents

Living archaeology

I first became interested in textile, craft and costume as a young child and have always been fascinated by the variety of materials and techniques used across time and around the world. Whether it was turning scraps of fabric into clothes for teddies, learning to spin fleece into yarn, or experimenting with foraged natural dyes over a campfire at the bottom of the garden, the connection between materials, processes and things has inspired me to keep learning new skills.

Studying archaeology at university and beyond, and working in the heritage industry has given me the opportunity to share traditional skills with others, and to recognise the place craftwork has in human development. I firmly believe that if we want to understand the potential of craft work today and gain insight into where it might be going in future years, we must understand where different techniques came from and how they reflect both the material culture of previous generations but also the landscape in which they developed. I often deliver demonstrations of ancient craft skills whilst wearing historical costume, at heritage sites, and this always generates discussions with visitors about just how skilled we are as a species, and how much of that is in danger of being lost.

Our current generations are from a world where machine made is the norm, and reclaiming an appreciation of aesthetically beautiful, highly functional but occasionally variable and imperfect (compared to their machine made equivalent) textile forms allows us to step back from the impersonable and embrace individual creativity. Working with natural materials and drawing on archaeological inspiration for projects is a key part of my own craft practice and one that I encourage others to explore.

Above: Working with plant fibres links us to traditions reaching back thousands of years

Left: Craft practice can link places as well as people, with projects reminding us of favourite locations

Right: Stone-Age techniques and materials can make objects that fit well into a modern lifestyle

PART ONE:
BACKGROUND AND BASICS

What exactly is nalbinding, what do we need and how do we get started? Getting a sense of the materials needed and the ways in which a project might be handled and finished puts us in a good place to start learning stitches in later chapters.

Nalbinding — it's not knitting!

There has been a great deal of confusion about the craft of nalbinding, and it is often mistakenly stated that it was the precursor to knitting and crochet. The byline of this book, *It's Not Knitting*, even resulted after a discussion between the publishers and me where they felt that associating nalbinding with knitting would help potential crafters to find the book, whilst I was keen that as a separate technique it should be treated as such!

Historical examples of nalbinding have often been misidentified as knitting, crochet, weaving or braiding, which causes confusion amongst collectors not used to analysing textiles. It is not until you try to recreate them that you realise that the structure is more closely related to knotting than to anything else. Knitting and crochet use a continuous length of yarn, which is drawn through previous stitches or sections, and which will generally unravel if the yarn is pulled before the work is fastened off, or if there is no hook or needle to stop it. Nalbinding is created stitch by stitch, usually with a needle, meaning that each loop is much more secure and the work difficult to undo except one loop at a time. Nalbinding occupies its own very special place in the crafting treasury. The superficial visual similarities between some nalbinding stitches and other techniques make it a valuable addition to a yarn-crafter's skillset.

Nalbinding has a surprisingly long history and geographic reach. Loop-manipulated textiles can be traced back into prehistory, and fragments survive from at least the Mesolithic period; however, it is likely that the craft predates any extant examples. Nalbinding is usually worked with the aid of one rather large needle, and covers the

Left: Yarn tied to weights on a warp-weighted loom

Below: Childrens' socks inspired by split-toe Egyptian socks (see project on page 71)

transition from plant to animal fibres and structures like practical bags and rugs as well as warm garments.

Versions of the technique can be found in the textile traditions of many cultures around the world. Sometimes it is found in highly practical items, such as the *bilum* bags of Papua New Guinea, milk strainers worked from cattle-hair cordage used until recently in Scandinavia, and camel muzzles from Oman. It is also used to make intricate clothing items, from cheerfully striped socks found in Egypt during late antiquity, to embroidered mittens that have become part of Sweden's folk costume tradition.

Despite this long pedigree, nalbinding has all but disappeared from the textile crafting repertoire of many regions. A resurgence in interest has been greatly assisted by the increase in internet-based resources, but it remains on the Heritage Crafts Red List of Endangered Crafts in Britain. Fortunately, it is easy to learn and extremely versatile, requiring nothing more than a suitable needle and some yarn.

A few contemporary practitioners will argue that not all loop-manipulated stitches are nalbinding, and may exclude the oldest forms of simple looping from their own practice. As a textile archaeologist, I respectfully disagree with them and, for our purposes, all loop-based stitches that are worked with the aid of a single needle and either relatively short lengths of yarn or by cord-as-you-go methods, are part of the same family of stitches. Exploring nalbinding therefore provides an opportunity to explore various eras and regions, and as we learn and practise different stitches, we will also look at the history of the different styles.

Let's start with the word itself. Contemporary English has no surviving word for this technique. We could say 'loop-manipulated stitches', but that's a bit of a mouthful. So, we have borrowed and somewhat Anglicised the Scandinavian term *nålbinding*, where there is a long and apparently unbroken tradition of the craft going back thousands of years. *Nål + binde* quite literally means 'needle binding', but you may also find it referred to as 'naalbinding', 'nalbinding', 'netless knotting', 'knotless netting', and many other things besides. Textile terminology often changes over time, and early texts frequently use different words to describe what we would today think of as nalbinding. This evolution of terms also means that when we say 'nalbinding needle' we are really saying 'a needle for needle binding'.

Because the broad technique has such a diverse history and geographical spread, it's likely that it has gone by many other names but, sadly, most of these are now lost to us. Throughout this book the simplified term 'nalbinding' will be used regardless of where or when inspiration is drawn from, and we will rely on the projects themselves to celebrate and reference the cultures that inspire them.

Where extant objects are used to inspire our projects, you'll find references to additional texts listed in the references and bibliography at the back of the book. Textile archaeology is a fast-moving field; new discoveries are made and ways of analysing existing finds are improved all the time, and I hope that this book will be a useful overview to those working from an academic perspective, as well as those wanting to develop new craft skills. Several key researchers have explored nalbinding over the years, from Daniel Davidson in the 1930s, Odd Nordland in the 1960s to Margrethe Hald in the 1980s. There are also numerous excellent current researchers worldwide including, to name just a couple, Anne Marie Decker who has made a detailed study of the many Egyptian socks amongst other items and Sanna-Mari Pihlajapiha who has done a great deal of work online to help people understand the Finnish traditions and stitches. Modern social media has allowed networking on an unprecedented scale, and there are now researchers, craftspeople, teachers and learners all exploring nalbinding globally and sharing their insights and projects. This book owes a great debt of thanks to all the people who have explored this technique in so much detail over the last century.

Below: Modern projects inspired by historic nalbinding: a phone case (see page 62) and a dice bag (see page 63)

A brief historical overview

The oldest currently known example of nalbinding is a fragment found in the Nehal Hemar cave in Israel, dated to approximately 6500 BCE (Barber 1991). These fragments include both simple and cross-knit stitches, and strongly suggest that the craft was already well developed by this date.

In Denmark, we have Mesolithic fragments from the waterlogged site of Tybrind Vig dating to around 4200 BCE (Andersen 2013) and several Neolithic fragments from the Circum-Alpine lake dwellings (Winiger 1981). All of these were made using plant fibres, and reflect a tradition of bast-fibre textile working that clearly predates the oldest surviving examples. It is not until the Bronze Age, centuries later, with the development of wool-coated sheep, that woollen yarns started to be woven on warp-weighted looms; at this point, we see a move away from techniques reliant on made-as-you-go cordage to ones that use pre-made yarns.

These techniques may have originally used thrums – lengths of warp thread left over after woven cloth is removed from the loom. Given how much time went into preparing wool and spinning it into yarn, these short lengths would have been far too valuable to discard. Although today we are much more likely to cut lengths from a ball of yarn when working a nalbound project, using these short sections of yarn is a reference to this thrifty and efficient use of resources.

Egypt's incredibly dry climate aids the preservation of fragile organic remains, and many examples of socks survive from late antiquity, worked in cross-knit looping and other stitches (Decker 2024). Neighbouring regions have given us incredibly detailed pieces such as the Dura-Europos fragments, worked a little before 256 CE in what is now Syria (Yale.edu. 2024).

Fast forward to the early medieval period and a wool sock from around 970 CE, found at the Coppergate site in York, England, has evidence of madder dye on the ankle; madder was one of the most popular dyestuffs of Viking-age Jorvik (Walton 1989). From tenth-century Mammen in Denmark there is evidence of a gold thread headband or covering (Hald 1980), and by the eleventh century we have mittens, represented by a surviving example from Oslo, and which has lent its name to one of the most popular nalbinding stitches.

Examples of European medieval socks include one from Uppsala and fragments from Kaukola in Finland, even a pair of linen stockings from Switzerland (Nordland 1961), although as far as we can tell the technique did not survive in the British Isles during this period.

Nalbinding is found on most continents. In Central America, where conditions for the preservation of archaeological textiles can sometimes be as good as they are in Egypt, a large quantity of fragments in cross-knit and simple looping variants have been found in the Paracas and Nazca textiles from Peru and the surrounding Andean region. In the south-west of America and northern Mexico, Pueblo shoe-socks were

Shoe-sock excavated in 1915 from the Two Mummy Cave Ruin, Arizona. Ancestral Pueblo (Anasazi), c. 1100–1300 CE.
Courtesy Arizona State Museum, The University of Arizona. Photographer, Jannelle Weakly

made by the Anasazi people, who worked rows of looping onto soles of braided yucca to create practical footwear.

Looped stitches technically related to nalbinding occur in the form of needle hitching in a variety of nautical contexts, where they are used to cover bottles or other objects, such as needle cases, and to provide filler stitches on decorative ropework. These techniques would have been familiar to many sailors over the last few hundred years, and are closely related to the oldest known nalbinding stitches. They can also be found as elements within embroidery and as a way of joining fabrics together, further blurring the lines between nalbinding stitches as stand-alone structures or as elements of other craft processes.

In Oman, the tradition of making camel muzzles and sand socks from nalbinding is still occasionally practised by men. This reminds us that material culture reflects societies and individuals as well as objective techniques; regional differences in gender

roles within textile manufacture help us understand the meaning and significance of those objects. Looking at how different societies approach techniques and their attitudes to the objects made from them can give us valuable insights into how similar objects may have fitted into societies that are now very distant from us in time.

In Africa, whole outfits made using looped structures have been associated with ritual dress, such as the dance costume shown here, and Congolese capes in intricately nalbound raffia fibre are marks of prestige (Decker 2024).

In Oceania, string bags, known as *bilum* in Papua New Guinea and *noken* in West Papua, have significant cultural importance. Made exclusively by women (MacKenzie 2019), they represent deeply embedded ideas and traditions that encompass gender roles and even the role of sorcery (Soukup 2023). As a practical craft form, they have also kept pace with changing times.

Recent anthropological studies have offered us potential insights into how similarly worked bags might have been made and used by people from different times and regions where the material culture is less well preserved. A wide variety of stitches have been traced to Oceania; many of these can be found worldwide, but a few, such as the hourglass pattern, are more specific to certain regions. The geographical diversity of these stitches strongly supports the idea of parallel development of disparate cultures across considerable periods of time.

Indigenous Australian people made dillybags using a variety of techniques, but simple looping and loop-and-twist is well represented (Davidson 1933), as is an efficient thigh-rolled cord-as-you-go technique.

Left: Man making a camel muzzle in Oman, 1992. © Pitt Rivers Museum, University of Oxford. Accession number: 2004.51.232

Right: Dance costume from the rite of passage of the Pende people of the Congo, mid 1800s. John Lee. National Museum Denmark

It would be easy to completely fill this book with more examples of nalbinding throughout the world and across time, but this is first and foremost a practical book, and one of the best ways to appreciate a technique is to go ahead and start working with it.

A note on terminology: Throughout this book we will use terms like yarn, thread, cord, string and twine. They can have specific meanings, but here we generally pick the one that best fits the project at hand. The important thing is to match the yarn to the project you have in mind.

Above: Pictured here are two *bilum* bags, one from the mid twentieth century, made from traditional local plant materials, and the other from the 1980s, made for functional use from repurposed synthetic fishing line and sold as a tourist souvenir. Both demonstrate a similar hourglass looping technique typical of the region; the more recent one has used the distinct colours to work dramatic patterns into the bag. Both in the collection of the author

Getting started

Nalbinding requires very little in the way of equipment to begin: some yarn and a large needle are all that is necessary. Before we start looking at stitches, let's look at choosing needles and yarn, and at yarn management and joining techniques.

Needles

Nalbinding is usually done with a relatively large, blunt needle (sometimes called a 'nal', even in English), but there are always exceptions to this. Some people like using a metal or plastic yarn needle, while others favour hand-carved needles in exotic woods, horn, antler or bone. Needles can be straight or curved, rustic or highly finished. In most cases, a smooth needle is better than one with a rough surface or too much carved decoration. Some have one large eye; others have more than one. It isn't hard to make a basic needle yourself using an old toothbrush, disposable bamboo cutlery or strips cut from an old credit card.

The eye needs to easily accommodate the yarn used, especially if you use more than one strand at once. If you are working a needle-tensioned stitch such as York or cross-knit looping, then the needle will determine the size of the stitches; if it is too large, it won't go through the available loops. Thumb-tensioned stitches such as Oslo or Dalby work well with largish needles, but you do need to be able to rotate them easily to pick up and manipulate stitches.

For this reason, it is quite common, even for beginners, to quickly accumulate a collection of needles, and for certain needles to become favourites. It is not at all unusual for nalbinders to find themselves adapting all sorts of things into needles, or looking out for sandpaper or a whittling knife to perfect the point on one that is almost, but not quite, right for a project.

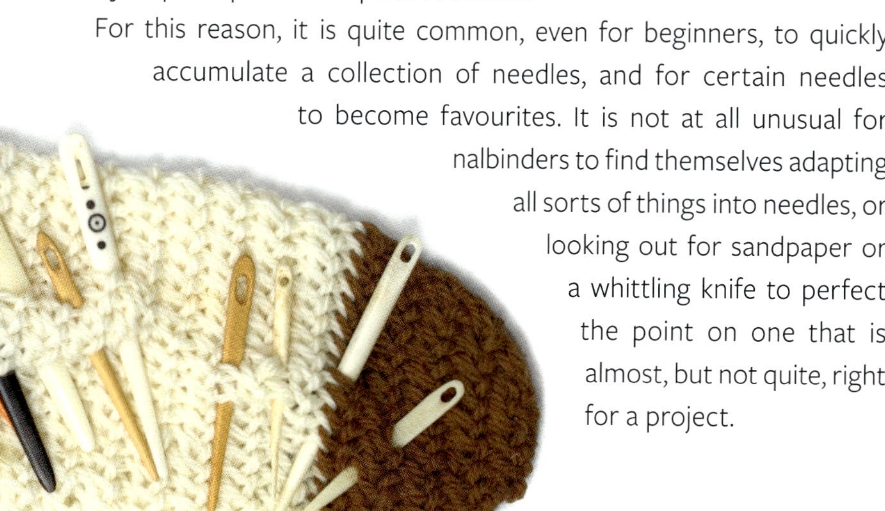

Below: **A sample swatch of nalbinding can make an excellent needle case, as can an odd nalbound sock**

Make your own nalbinding needle

You will need:

- a piece of wood about as long as your index finger (your 'blank'). This could be a lollipop stick, a piece cut from a bamboo toothbrush, a stick from a suitable tree with a dense grain or a slim piece of hardwood from a model-making supply shop. For many people, making use of foraged or found materials is half the fun;

- a drill and some sandpaper (a saw or sharp knife is useful if repurposing things like old toothbrushes, but you can do a lot just with sandpaper or a coarse nail file).

Above: **Needle-making materials**

A

B

1. First, mark then drill the hole (**A**). This way, if the hole ends up slightly off-centre, you can finish the needle to suit rather than having a finished needle with the hole not quite where you wanted it. A largish round eye is fine if your blank has room for it, but if you prefer an oval hole, drill two or three smaller holes close together, then use a little folded sandpaper or a small file to smooth out the inside of the hole until it is even.

2. When you are happy with the eye, finish shaping the rest of your needle (**B**). Aim for something that feels nice in your fingers. Your needle needn't be perfectly straight, and most nalbinders end up with several different sizes to suit different projects.

3. Check that the point isn't too sharp; many yarns that are good for nalbinding are softly spun, and very pointy needles can split yarn loops at unwanted moments. A slightly blunt point is generally easier to work with, and you'll be able to refine the point to suit your own tastes as you become more used to working the different stitches.

4. Finish up with the finest grade of sandpaper you have available, and then use a drop of oil or a little wax to bring out the natural beauty of your needle. You'll also find that the natural oils from your hands will continue to polish and improve your needle as you use it.

Yarn

Nalbinding can be done with a very wide range of yarns and yarn-like materials, from raffia strands or lime bast to handmade cordage, fine, smooth cotton or linen to rough, hairy garden twine, and smoothly spun, plied yarn to lofty and lightly twisted roving-style yarn.

Although a lot of modern nalbinding is done in relatively bulky yarn, in centuries past we are as likely to find very fine, dense work. The beauty of this technique is its adaptability to the materials at hand. You can work the same stitch in a very open way or pull it tight and close for a completely different effect.

The key decision when choosing a yarn is how you intend to join the lengths together. You might find that some of the more complex thumb-tensioned stitches are more elegantly achieved with yarns that can be spliced or felted together, whereas rustic plant-fibre yarns work very well in some of the oldest stitches, such as simple looping or looping around a core. Don't rule out combining yarn types in a project: working with different thicknesses, textures and materials can result in exciting and artistic results. Try looping a soft, bright yarn around a heavy string core to create bold, three-dimensional structures or mats.

Hand-spun yarn is usually excellent for nalbinding as you have control over the finished structure of the yarn and can match it to the intended project, but if you are new to the craft you may want to save yarns with a variable thick and thin texture until you have mastered a particular stitch.

Consider the end use of your project. If it's something like a hat or scarf that benefits from being light and

Above: **Bright dishcloth cotton, plied pure wool yarn and roving-style yarn are all excellent yarns to start with**

fluffy, then the thick, loosely twisted roving-style yarns are an excellent choice. Mittens that will be fulled are also excellent in this style of yarn, or to retain more stitch definition choose a plied yarn. Socks and slippers take a lot of wear and tear, so the more robust the yarn the more long wearing they will be. You may also want to work the stitches a little more densely to further increase wear.

Most of the projects in this book are worked using either plant fibres for the very earliest stitches, or a plied aran-weight or bulky roving-style yarn for the wool projects.

Basic skills

et's have a quick look at some of the techniques and terminology that you will encounter in the next two sections of this book. Some of them may not make much sense until you start to work with the stitches, but putting these all together here means you can revisit them to help refine your technique as your skills grow.

Yarn management

Unlike knitting, crochet, weaving, tatting and many other yarn crafts, nalbinding is usually done with relatively short lengths of yarn. There is almost always a balancing act between using lengths long enough to allow you to work without rejoining for a while, and fitting that length into your needle or through the stitches of your project.

When you start learning, use pieces of yarn just one or two arms' length for your first attempts. This lessens the risk of getting tangled up, and if you decide a practise piece has gone as far as it can, you won't have wasted yarn. If using a yarn that will felt, break it rather than cutting it with scissors. This makes it easier to make a felted join. If the yarn is hard to break, try gripping it with your hands further apart; sometimes that allows the strand to break at the fibre's natural staple length.

Below: Chains of stitches made when learning to nalbind can easily be turned into apparently more complex braids

Joining in new yarn

Felted join

This is one of the most common joining methods when using yarn that will easily felt. It is sometimes, rather less elegantly, called a 'spit splice' because it is possible to lick the yarn rather than dip it in water, but for this demonstration let us be genteel.

1. If you don't already have a soft end from snapping the yarn apart, it can help to fluff up the last few millimetres to increase surface area (**A**). If your yarn is thick and made up of several plies, you may wish to unravel the plies for a few twists and clip away a strand or two so that the finished join is of the same thickness as the original yarn.

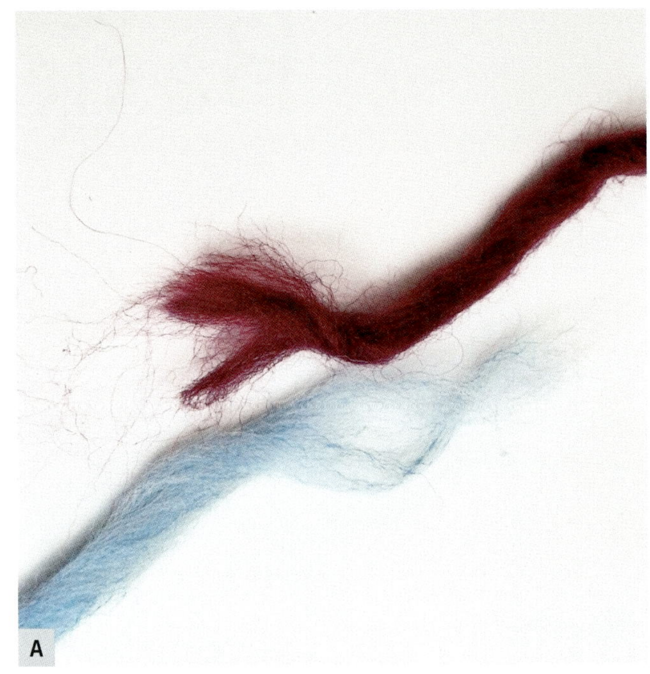

2. Moisten the two ends of the yarn to be joined together. You could dip it in water or use a small spray bottle, which is convenient and portable.

3. Overlap the damp edges, then put the join between the palms of your hand (**B**).

4. Rub the ends together hard and fast, applying pressure. You should find the ends of yarn felt together quite fast (**C**), but be aware that some yarns take a bit more rubbing than others.

5. If the yarns are of different colours, you will usually notice a graduated or even a barley-twist effect at the join (**D**). This can make for interesting transitions between shades, but if you prefer clean transitions, you can avoid the overlap effect by folding the ends of the yarn back on themselves before felting (see Russian join, Step 1).

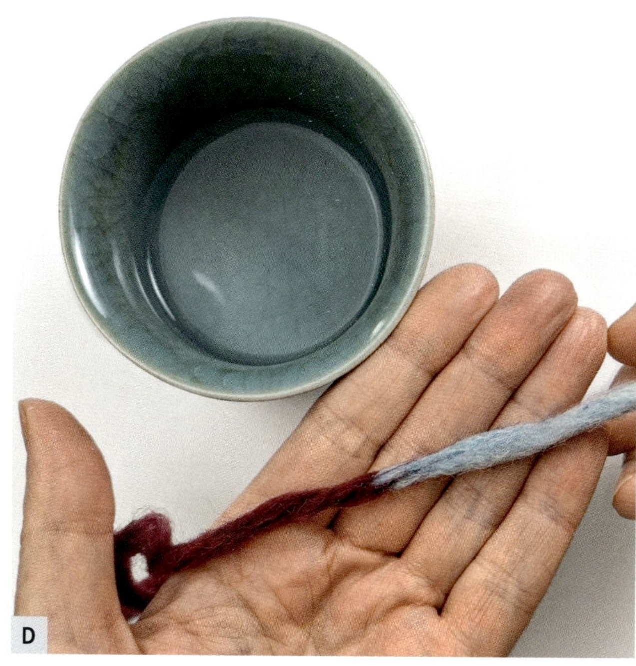

Russian join

For plied yarn that doesn't felt easily, such as super-wash-treated wool or acrylic, this method overlaps two yarns then sews the ends back into the yarn to create a secure join. It is worth practising a couple of times before using it in a project, but once you have the hang of it is a very neat way to join yarns, and creates a sharp transition between colours. You will need a needle with a reasonably slim shaft and sharp point, such as a darning needle.

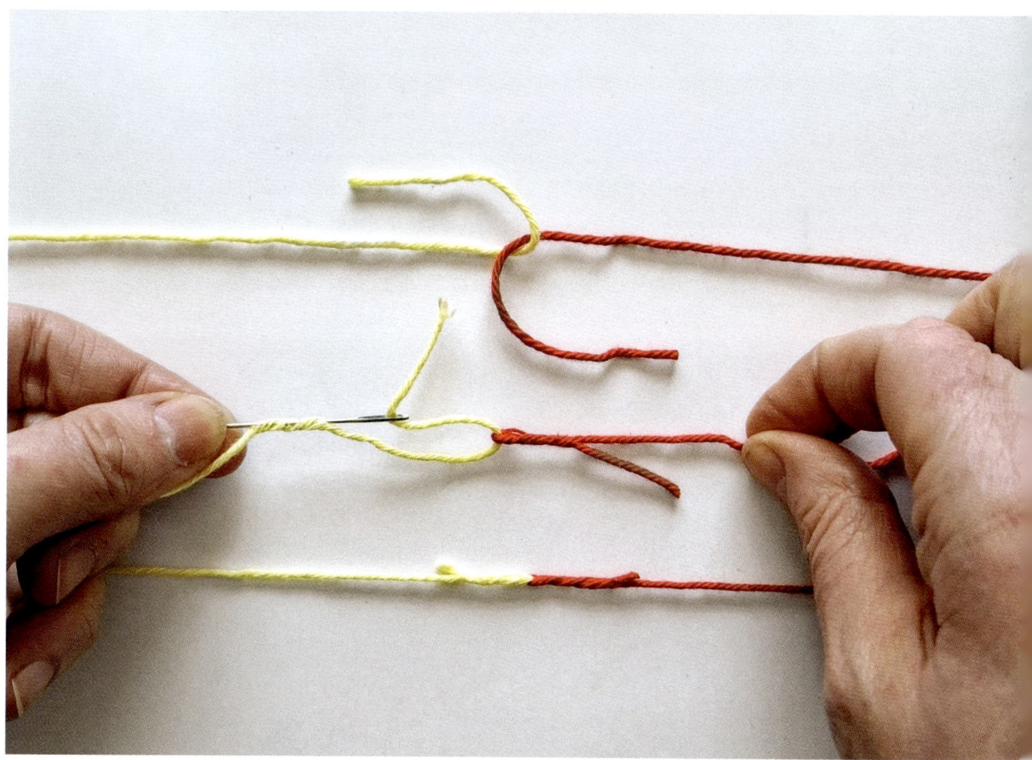
Above: **Working the Russian join**

1. Cross the ends of the yarns to be joined and fold them back on themselves.

2. Thread one end into the needle and wriggle the point through the plies of the yarn a few times.

3. Pull gently to close the loop and smooth down the join.

4. Repeat on the other piece of yarn.

5. Roll the join briefly between your fingers to smooth everything into place, then clip off the ends.

Overlapped join

This is a useful method for firm or stiff yarns. It is sometimes called a 'lazy join', though there is nothing lazy about using the most efficient join for your project.

If it is not practical to join the ends of two lengths of yarn together, you can lay the new one against the current row of stitches and work over it for a short distance, then swap the new yarn for the tail of the old one, working over that for a few more stitches to secure it. In this example, two different yarns were used for clarity in a simple looping stitch. The blue yarn is worked over until the linen yarn starts to run out, then their places are swapped, and the blue becomes the working yarn.

On the next round, any remaining tails can be worked over to hide them or, if the work is secure enough already, they can be clipped off with scissors.

In stitches like looping over a core, this join is essentially invisible, and it also works well with dense stitches like York where it can be used decoratively. Swapping back and forth between two shades and carrying the other inside the stitches allows you to do counted colourwork.

Felting-needle join

For really tricky fibres, or for wool that, for whatever reason, absolutely refuses to felt, a barbed felting needle can be used to entangle the fibres. These needles are used in modern industrial felting processes and have become popular with crafters for needle-felted sculpture or art. We can use them to mesh yarns that won't join in other ways. You probably won't need this tactic often, but it can be a useful skill. All you need to do is overlap the ends as for a felted join, then repeatedly stab the area with the felting needle, occasionally rearranging the yarn to bring any unworked areas to the top, until the join is secure. Do use a piece of foam to work against and mind your fingers – felting needles are wickedly sharp.

Working the overlapped join

Working the felting-needle join

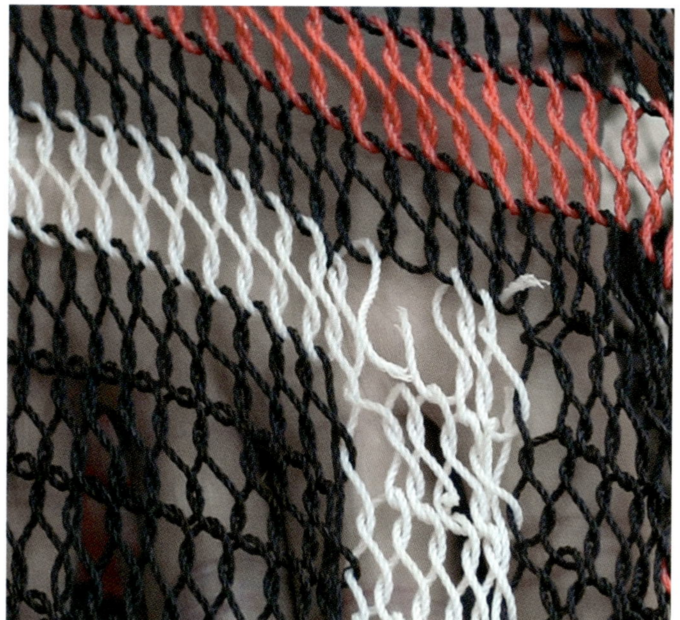

The fishing line in this *bilum* bag has been joined with overhand knots

The 'magic knot' (upper) and Weaver's Knot (lower) both make neat, generally stable knots in all but the slickest yarn

Knots

Joining your yarn with a knot is occasionally necessary. In this *bilum* bag from Papua New Guinea the synthetic fishing line yarn has been joined with overhand knots, but a small area shows where a knot has failed, and the work is slightly unravelling. In a springy, slippery material like this, the knot is still probably the most secure option.

Knitters and crocheters often use something they call a 'magic knot', which creates a reliable knot with a small surface area. Another knot worth trying out is the Weaver's Knot.

The 'magic knot' is made by tying a simple overhand knot in each tail of yarn so that it captures the opposing yarn. Tighten the knots, then draw them together by pulling on the yarns. Pull the knot tight and roll it between your fingers to check that it is secure before clipping off the ends.

The Weaver's Knot is very easy to tie and is a good option where there won't be much strain on the yarn. It is essentially the same as the sheet bend knot used in netmaking and is worked by folding one yarn end into a loop then passing the other yarn end up through this loop, behind both 'legs' of it, then tucking the end through. Pull to tighten, and the knot should form securely.

In both cases, either clip the ends or for even more security leave them long to be woven in at the end of the project.

Working the 'magic knot'

Working the Weaver's Knot

Threading and holding the needle

As you gain experience with working the stitches you will find you are comfortable handling longer lengths of yarn, and it's worth trying different methods of managing lengths for efficient and comfortable working.

How you hold the needle is more about personal preference than there being any right or wrong way, but do try to develop movements that don't have you gripping the needle too tightly or you will tire more quickly.

There are several ways to thread a needle for nalbinding, aside from the obvious one. If the eye of the needle is large enough you may be able to fit several folds of yarn through it at once. This will minimise the length of yarn you have to pull through each stitch as you make it, speeding up your work. If your needle has more than one hole, you can use this to carry extra lengths of yarn too.

Above: **A loaded needle**

Chain-plying

Chain-plying is a very effective tactic, and you can use it to fit three times as much yarn into a length as usual.

1. Make a loose finger-crochet chain of yarn (**A**).

A

2. Thread the starting end and first loop into the needle eye (**B**).

3. As you work, you can gently pull on the chain to undo one loop at a time from the bottom where it joins your work. Don't worry about making the loops perfectly even; it's the structure of this method that makes it work, not how tidily you do it.

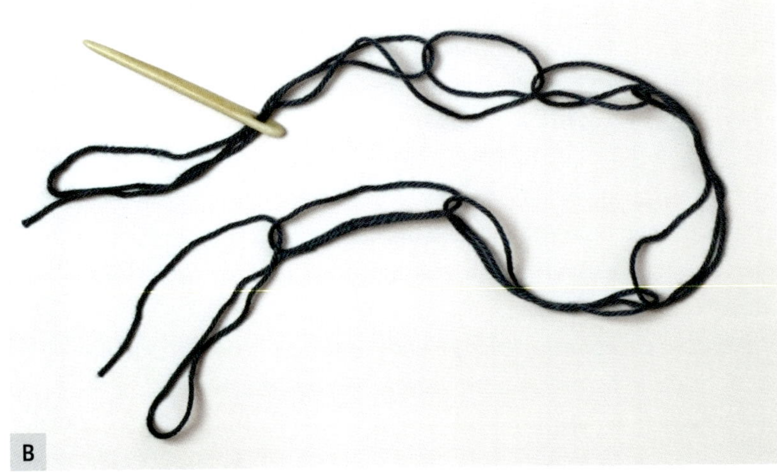

B

Tensioning the yarn

Almost everybody worries about their work looking messy at the starting point. This is because it often takes a few stitches for the loops to settle down to the right size, especially if you start with a loose overhand knot in your yarn rather than wrapping around the thumb. The good news is that this is very easy to resolve.

For projects that begin with a starting chain of a certain length, work a few stitches then unpick the very first few loops until you are happy with the tension. Carry on with your starting chain until it is long enough to work with. The first few loops can also be gently tightened by hand to create a tapered start if that suits your project better.

Above: **The ideal position for the thumb loops is around the base of your thumbnail**

Some stitches are relatively easy to keep at a consistent size because you always form the loops around the base of the thumbnail, but even then it is important to tighten the same amount and use the same part of the thumb as the gauge. If you are working a thumb-tensioned stitch and are not happy with the regularity of your stitches, take a good look at where your new loop forms. For most people, the optimum place is around the base of the thumbnail (see **A**), but if your particular hand shape or preferred working position means that you tend to form the stitch elsewhere on the thumb, that is absolutely fine; just take a note of where, and aim to use the same place with the new loop pulled up to the same tension each time.

Usually, working a length of chain or a very simple project with no aim other than to perfect your tension will get things behaving very quickly.

It is also possible to reduce the size of thumb-tensioned stitches. This is particularly useful at the end of a piece of work where you may want to reduce the size systematically over three or four stitches to create an elegant taper at the finish, rather than an abrupt step. Simply drop the thumb loop off the thumb after you form it, and gently pull it a little tighter before making the next stitch. Pinch the adjusted loop between thumb and forefinger to keep it in place as you work.

If you plan to work a thumb-tensioned stitch but want the whole project to have smaller loops, you can tension on the needle instead of the thumb. This is a useful method for people with joint conditions who find it hard to keep loops even on the thumb. Choose a needle with a regular shape and the diameter of the desired stitch size. This is very much like choosing the right hook or needles in crochet or knitting. The method is shown here, using Oslo stitch.

1. Make your first stitch or two over the thumb to get things started (**A**).

2. Drop the thumb loop onto the needle and gently pull the working thread until the loop closes to the right size (**B**).

3. Finish pulling the thread through to complete the stitch, and this motion will create the new thumb loop ready to be moved onto the needle for tensioning (**C**). Once you get into a rhythm, the main difference with this method is that your old thumb loop will now be sitting as a rear loop and will need picking up from behind your thumb rather than sitting ready on its tip (**D**).

For stitches that are not formed around the thumb and that rely on pulling loops to the desired size, such as York or cross-knit looping, it can be very useful to match your needle to the project. If your needle fits comfortably through each loop as you work into it, you will quickly notice if things are becoming harder to pull through or if more space is forming. Again, a little practise usually resolves this.

Understanding the patterns

I will go through the main points again as we come to them in the stitch instructions, but most of the projects in this book start by suggesting a type of yarn, a stitch and possible joining methods.

Although some projects may say how many stitches or rows went into the sample, it's important to use these as broad guidelines, so don't worry if your tension, yarn or working style means you need to work a row or two extra or fewer to get the same effect. It is useful to first try some of the projects exactly as written to get an idea of how it all works, but be ready to work intuitively when you start developing your own ideas.

Working flat

Nalbinding is most often worked in the round as a tube or spiral; it is possible to work most of the stitches flat, although some are easier than others.

Making turning stitches

Working flat usually requires a turning stitch or two to be made at the end of the row to allow the first stitch of the next row to be made.

- In needle-tensioned stitches such as York or cross-knit looping, a simple loop added at the end of a row might be enough to allow you to turn your work (**A**).

- Thumb-tensioned stitches such as Oslo generally work better if you make an additional two-stitch chain at the end of the row, then turn and work into the first stitch of the actual row (**B**).

- If you turn and work back without a turning strategy you may find your work narrows by a stitch on each row, resulting in uneven work. This can be a useful technique for creating a gradually tapering strip of fabric.

It is also possible to work a tube in the round then cut it open to create a flat piece of fabric. Like steeking in knitting, this is more stable than it sounds. Because nalbinding is fundamentally a series of knots, there isn't much to unravel. It may look a little alarming at first, but you can turn the cut edges of a piece to the inside of a project and work an edge over them (**C**).

Connecting stitches

Regardless of whether you work in the round or flat, you will need to join new stitches to the row below. Nalbinding notations refer to the point at which you join new stitches as F1, F2, B1, B2, M1 and so on. The letters tell you where a join is made, i.e., from the front, back or middle of the loops, and the numbers refer to the number of loops you pick up as you go.

F connections

An F1 or F2 connection is common on thumb-tensioned stitches such as Oslo or Mammen and is very easy to make. Here they are shown in Oslo stitch.

- F1: When you are ready to join to the row beneath, put the needle through the first available loop (**A**). The needle is pointing away from you as you do this.

- F2: Put the needle through the next loop <u>and</u> the one behind it (**B**). This may already have a stitch going through it.

B connections

Connecting stitches through the back is a little less common but may still be useful.

- B1: Put the needle through the back of the top loop of the next stitch in the previous row (C). The needle is pointing towards you as you do this. The result is a little tighter than the F1 connection.

- B2: The needle goes through the back of the loop behind and the next loop with the needle coming towards you (D). Think of this as F2 worked back to front.

M connections

On thumb-tensioned stitches such as Oslo there is a middle stitch that lies in the opposite direction from the top loops.

- M1: Put the needle through the front of the middle loop (E). This results in a very dense fabric as the top edge of the stitch will fold to the inside of the work.

Shaping your work

Increases and decreases

There are relatively few variations in increase or decrease methods.

- Increases are generally worked by making two stitches in the same place (**A**).

- Decreases require either working two loops together into one stitch or missing a loop (**B**).

Fulling

If your yarn will felt, fulling provides additional options for shaping and finishing your project. Fulling is the action of felting a completed fabric. A finished nalbound piece of work can be washed and agitated in warm soapy water until the fibres tangle together and it shrinks, getting denser in the process. This can be done very slightly to perfect the fit of a hat, or very firmly for weatherproof mittens or cosy slippers.

Fulling is very easy to do by hand if your yarn felts easily. For larger projects you might consider machine washing, but you will not have as much control over the results, which is very important if you are aiming for a specific size or want a particular surface finish.

Above: Two very similar samples worked in Oslo stitch, using a roving-style yarn

1. Fill a bowl with water as hot as you can safely handle (**A**).

2. Immerse your project and give it a good rub with soap or a squeeze of washing up liquid (**B**).

3. Knead, rub, roll and wring your project in the hot soapy water until it has shrunk as much as you require (**C**, **D**, **E**). Keep changing the direction of work to make sure it shrinks evenly.

4. When it has shrunk enough, rinse it very thoroughly and pat into shape. Allow to dry completely.

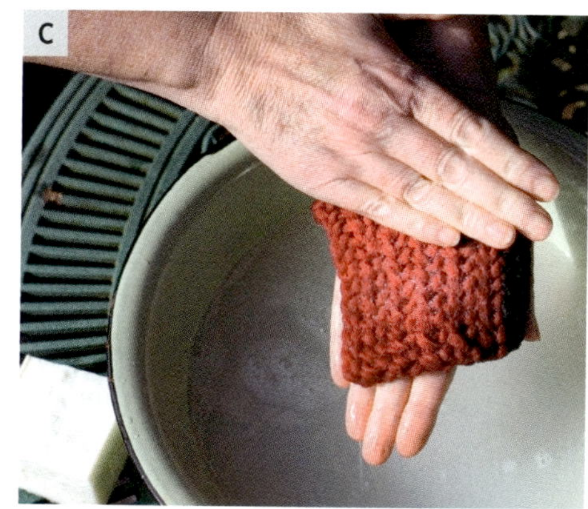

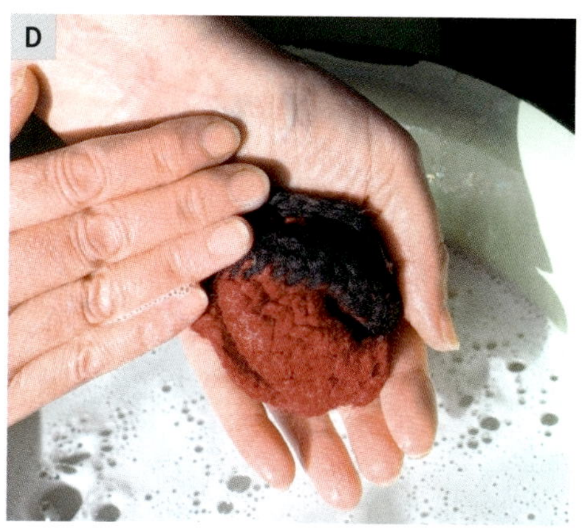

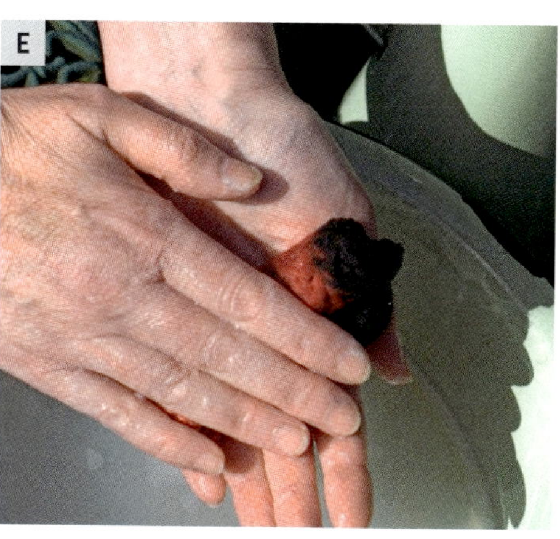

Above: The sample has been fulled enough to firm and shrink it but not so much that the original stitch definition is lost.

Above right: Finishing smaller stitches

Finishing

When you reach the end of a piece of work, you will need to deal with your last active stitch. In many cases, the simplest way to finish is to make the last stitch or two smaller than usual so that the work tapers off neatly; the ends can then be threaded through the remaining loops and sewn in. This is particularly useful if working in the round.

Left-handed working

Most of the illustrations in this book are from the perspective of a right-handed worker, but generally the only difference to the written instructions for left-handed users will be to reverse clockwise and anticlockwise directions, effectively mirroring the work. Here, I've provided a full description of Oslo stitch with photos from the left-handed perspective to get left-handed readers off to a good start.

Left-handed Oslo stitch

1. Use a piece of yarn once or twice the length of your arm and either make a loose overhand knot in one end of it or wrap the yarn around your thumb to form a loop.

2. Position this loop at the base of your thumbnail, so that you can lightly pinch the knot between your finger and thumb. The working end of the thread should be coming over the V between finger and thumb (**A**). This is your thumb loop (TL).

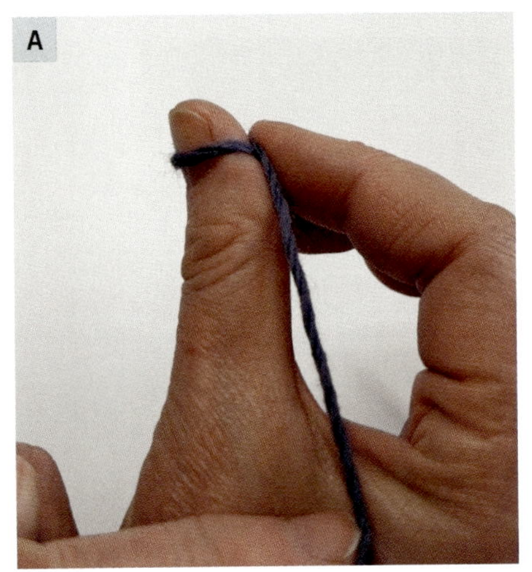
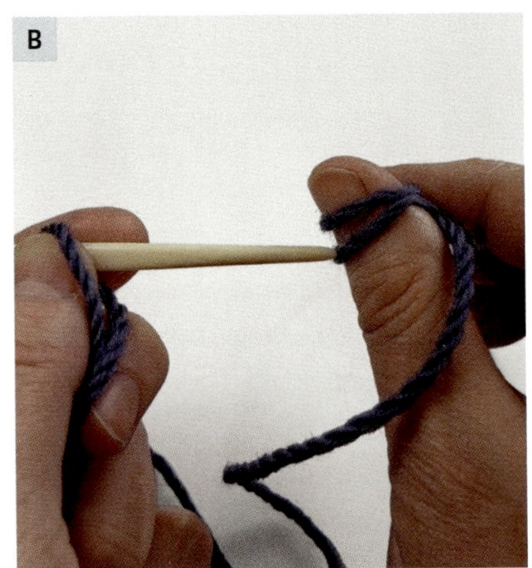

3. Take the point of the needle and put it through the TL at the point where you are pinching it, working under both threads. This is often called the 'cross'. The needle is pointing towards the V of your hand.

4. Pull the needle through, over the V in your hand, forming a second loop. Watch that it doesn't jump off your thumb tip as you pull.

5. You want this new loop to sit below the old TL, ideally around the base of your thumbnail (**B**).

6. This set-up creates the two loops necessary for Oslo stitch. From here on, two main motions form each stitch.

7. Use the point of the needle to gently push the old TL (nearest the tip of your thumb) off so it becomes

a rear loop (RL). Leave the needle in place, poking through the loop (**C**). You will put the needle tip through this point in the next step.

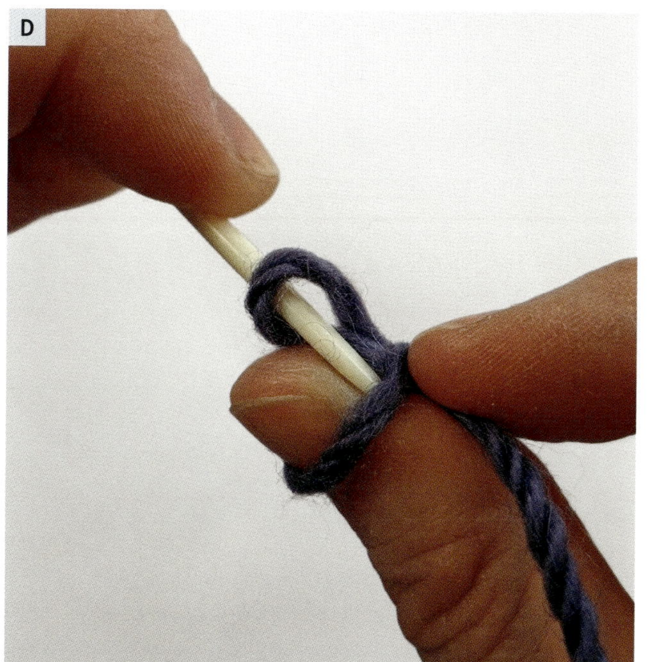

8. Rotate the needle with the RL clockwise so that it goes over the edge of the RL until you can insert it behind the cross, where it is being pinched between thumb and index finger (**D**). Then pull the yarn through to create the new TL below the old one (**E**).

9. Repeat these two motions until you have a chain of stitches (**F**). Don't worry if this looks like a loopy caterpillar at this stage!

10. Pull gently on the end of the chain and it will settle into even loops (**G**).

Planning a project

Above: **Stitch markers and hair clips are very useful for keeping your place**

Throughout this book, I have used projects to help explore the practicalities and effects of each stitch. This quick overview will run through some of the factors that go into planning a project, and will help you to consider the different elements of a project when you start designing your own.

- The yarn you will be using and how much of it you will need: try to match yarn to function; a delicate, airy scarf can use a light yarn, but socks need something more hardwearing if they are going to last.

- Making sure it will fit: nalbinding is highly variable, and the combination of yarn, needle and tension can affect it. The safest way to plan a project that needs to have a certain fit is to make a sample piece using the same yarn and stitch and do some simple calculations to check you are working with the right number of stitches.

- Taking measurements and trying things on as you go: if you make your first project to fit either yourself or someone you know well, and who can try the work on as it progresses, you will quickly get an idea of how sizing works. It then becomes easier to use measurements to scale another project to suit a child or someone with a very different body shape to your own.

- Work pairs of items together: because nalbinding is highly intuitive, it is much easier to make each one of a pair of socks or mittens at the same time. That way, whatever you decide is needed for the shaping, you can immediately replicate on the other one of the pair without needing to try to remember later what you were thinking.

- The nature of nalbinding: work with it rather than expecting it to behave like knitting or crochet. Some stitches will have similarities, but most are very individual. This means you can combine stitches in a project to create unique effects.

- Stretch: in most cases, nalbinding projects will stretch lengthways when worn or when wet. This means you need to be a bit careful when putting on or taking off socks and mittens, and may need to allow a little negative ease (i.e., make items a fraction shorter than looks right) to compensate for this.

- Working in the round vs working flat: working in the round is usually easier than working flat, but flat has its place too.

- Know your place: mark the start of a round with a scrap of contrasting yarn or stitch marker. The types sold for use in crochet are very useful, but household objects like paper clips can do the same job.

- Park your work: if leaving your work for the day, a spring hairclip is very useful for holding your loops in position.

How to use this book

Be intuitive! That may sound like an odd thing to write in a how-to book, but one of the great advantages of nalbinding is that it lends itself to working beyond a pattern. Because stitches will vary in size according to your tension, needle size and yarn type, it is very hard to write precise patterns for nalbound projects. In many cases you can add shaping as you see fit, switch between suitable stitches, and design as you work.

As a result, in this book you will find 'recipes' for projects rather than patterns. These will often include the number of stitches used in the sample project pictured, but will encourage you to try on your work regularly (if it is something like a hat or sock) and to make any necessary adjustments.

The intuitive nature of nalbinding increases and decreases makes it the perfect craft for anyone who dislikes following rigid patterns. It is much more a case of 'do this until it's wide enough, then do that until it's long enough', and you can add your own creative twists as you go along.

For crafters coming from a more structured knitting or crochet background, this can at first seem imprecise and a little nerve wracking, but it is also very liberating, allowing you to be truly creative with just a single needle and a few lengths of yarn.

Each stitch tutorial has a project or two explained in detail to help you see the potential and limitations, but there is also a final section that looks at socks in more detail and which suggests a range of stitches and shaping strategies to use as the basis for your own creations. As you become more practised at reading your work, you will be able to estimate increases based on whether your stitches are lying at a slant or perpendicular to the row below and will hardly need anything more than a rough idea of the shape you want your project to take.

Above all, have fun with it! Nalbinding rewards the time taken to experiment, make mistakes and learn your own unique ways of working. As you explore it, you will be continuing a tradition of textile working that has been with us for well over 8,500 years, and helping it survive for the next generation of craft workers.

PART TWO:
NEEDLE-TENSIONED STITCHES

The oldest nalbinding stitches currently known all rely on the loops being tightened to the desired size once the needle has passed through the stitch. Using a needle that fits the loop helps ensure consistent results.

Simple looping

Examples of simple looping and closely related techniques can be found in all regions of the world where there is evidence of nalbinding. Often referred to as 'knotless netting' by early researchers, the worldwide distribution of such examples, often in the form of bags, strongly suggests that this technique developed independently in many different areas across millennia. Today, you will occasionally hear simple looping called 'Danish stitch', and those of you that sew or embroider will be familiar with its structure in the form of blanket stitch.

The oldest fragments of loop-manipulated fabrics date back around 8,500 years to the Mesolithic era and are made from plant fibres. It is very likely that all looping methods develop as a progression from cord-making, creating cord as the project progresses rather than cutting a complete ball of string into shorter sections.

Today, simple looping is an elegant and straightforward stitch to learn, and can be used to create fabrics with multi-dimensional stretch that can be dense and firm or lacy and open. It is an easy stitch to modify by adding twist to the loops, as you can see in this fragment of a Neolithic carrying net or bag from Switzerland. In this image, it is possible to see where a drawstring or foundation loop pulls the lowermost loops together.

Choosing fibres

Modern crafters are used to obtaining all the materials for a project in one go, and this approach may look a little awkward at first. It is, however, remarkably efficient, allowing the maker to create exactly what they need without having to join in ends. It is also a fantastic way to use repurposed, recycled or foraged fibres, allowing the creation of thick or thin cordage that exactly suits the project.

Flax or hemp fibres are ideal for trying out looped stitches, as are foraged fibres like nettle, lime bast, horseradish or even rhubarb! Raffia is available from most craft suppliers.

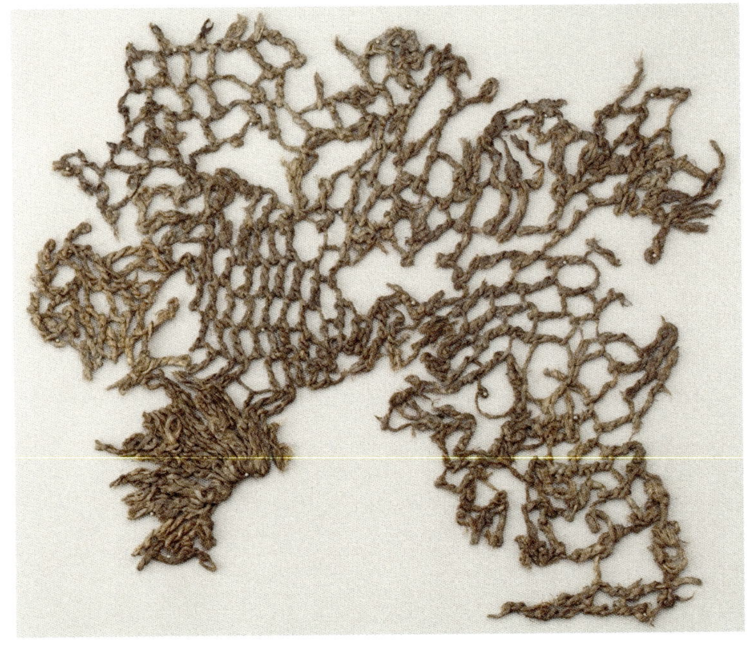

Below: Assorted fragments of a carrying net, Horgen Culture (between 3500 and 2850 BCE) Feldmeilin, Switzerland.
© Kantonsarchäologie Zürich, Photographer Martin Bachmann

Tutorials for obtaining a wide range of plant fibres without damaging the environment are available online, and as appropriate species will vary with area, you can plan projects that reflect your local landscape. If you don't have access to plant fibres but want to try these projects, you could try using fine strips of lightly moistened paper, which can make a very substantial string.

Some people prefer to work plant fibres while they are slightly damp, but don't be tempted to over wet them; in most cases, all you need to do is moisten your fingertips or wrap a small amount of fibre in a damp cloth while working to make it supple and easy to twist. Some, more robust, fibres need a little more wetting, but this almost never means actual soaking.

Whatever fibre you choose, plant fibres have a subtle palette of shades of pale gold, silvery grey, soft green and red, which all blend together well and give a beautifully natural feel to your work.

We'll start by taking the technique back to its roots and will look at looping using handmade cordage.

Making cord

1. Start by selecting a small bundle of fibres roughly half as thick as the desired cord. In this case I have used hemp fibres (**A**).

2. Hold the bundle near the middle in your non-dominant hand and use the dominant one (in these pictures this is the right hand) to twist the fibres away from you in a clockwise direction (**B**).

3. As soon as the twist makes the fibre buckle, fold the bundle in half and you should start to see the beginnings of a piece of two-ply cord (**C**).

4. Twist the top bundle away from you, then bring it over the top of the lower one and towards you so that they swap places. Use the non-dominant hand to gently pinch the crossover point to help keep it organised (**D**).

5. Now there is a new top strand. Repeat the pattern of twisting the top strand away from you then crossing it over and down until you are nearly at the end of your bundle of fibre (**E**).

6. To join in more fibre, use just a very few strands of fibre (much less than in your original bundle) and lay it across both strands so it extends to each side (**F**). As you start twisting again this will seamlessly join the existing cord. Add a few fibres as often as needed to maintain your chosen thickness and continue until you have at least an arm's length of cord.

Tips

- Keep your grip light; the supporting hand can let go at any point and is only there to help control the twist.

- You can stop, put things down or rearrange your hands at any time.

- Don't over twist each time; you only need enough twist to allow the cord to form as you cross over the strands.

- Efficient motions mean you'll be able to work without tiring your hands.

Simple looping over foundation row

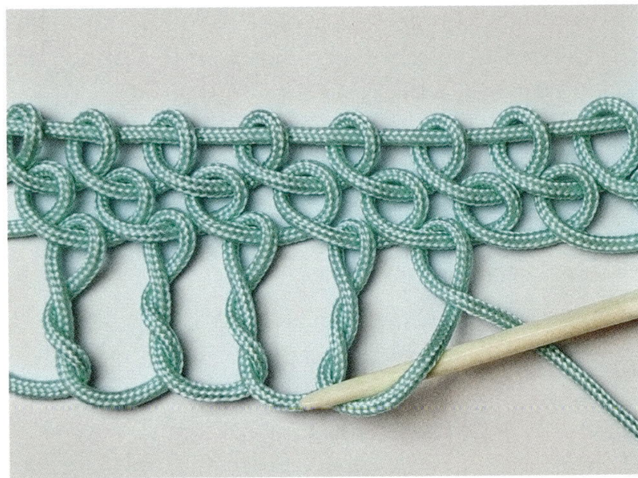

Looping with a twist

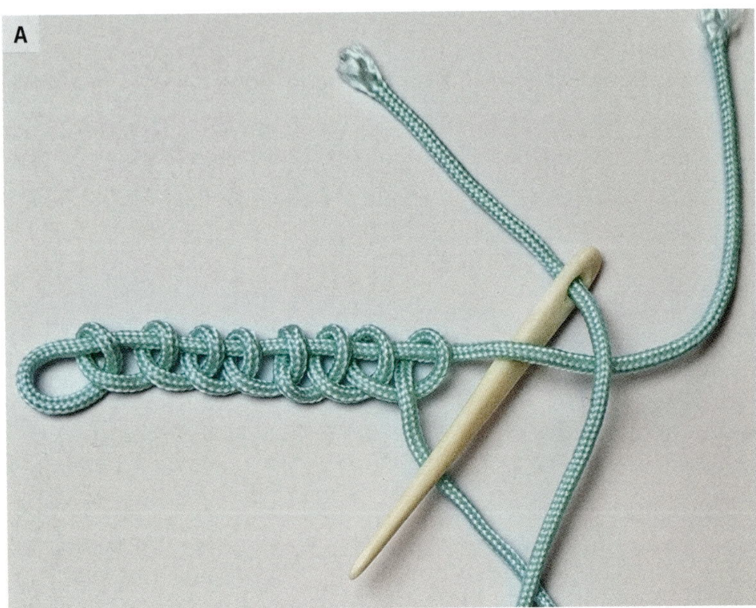

Simple looping, looping around a core and loop-and-twist stitch

The samples pictured show the differences between the simplest possible loop stitch worked over a foundation cord in the top row, and a variation with an extra twist.

Looping around a core adds a passive element (the core) that is worked over in each stitch; the foundation row in **A** and **B** is technically a core as well as a supporting cord. In **A**, the tail is of the same yarn as the core (the straight line of yarn running through the centre of the stitches). In **B**, a contrasting yarn is used as the core on the second row. In both cases, the simple loops encase the core, but the technique used to form the stitch itself remains the same. We will look at this technique in the following sections.

A round start using cord-as-you-go

The round start illustrated here is an essential technique in nalbinding, regardless of whether you make the cord yourself or work with a ball of yarn. We will revisit this technique as we look at different stitches, but here we are using the starting point of the handmade cordage as a key element in setting up the work.

I recommend making at least an arm's length of cord before you start a project; if it is too long it can be awkward to pull through the loops, so it is best to add cordage to the end steadily as your work progresses.

1. Start by finding the loop that formed when you folded your original bundle of fibres in half to begin the cordage (**A**).

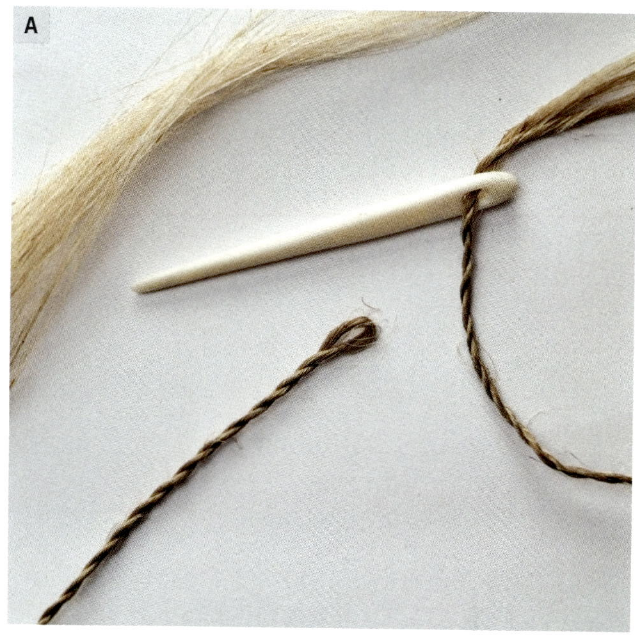

2. Thread the live end of the cord through this loop. Observe how it pulls up into a sliding loop or snare (**B**). I believe it is highly likely that our prehistoric ancestors first observed the usefulness of this sliding loop when developing hunting strategies in the distant past.

3. Pull the loop up until it is just big enough that you can poke the tip of your finger through it. This will become the centre of your round start, and we will be working simple loops into it.

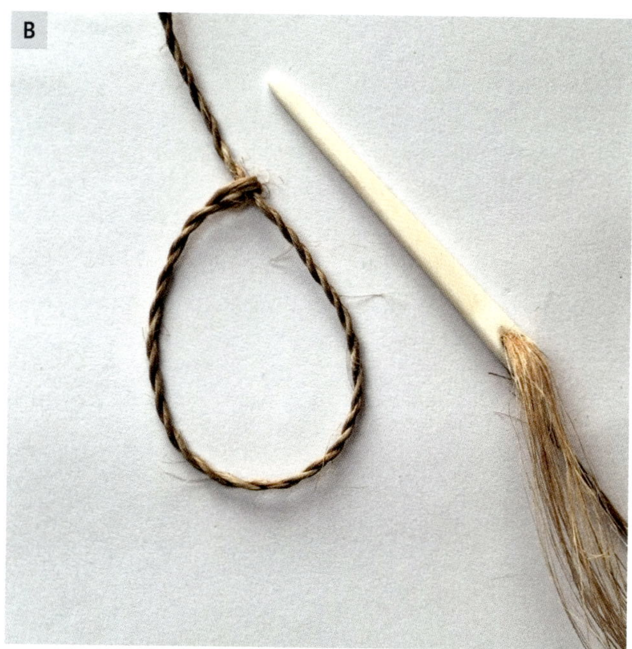

4. The stitches we will be making are essentially blanket stitch. If it helps, thread your cord onto a needle, but it is also frequently possible to work without a needle, especially when using stiffer plant fibres.

5. For right-handed working, arrange the start so that it looks a little like a number six, with the cord coming up from the top and trailing towards your working hand (**C**). For left-handers, think of it as looking like the lower case 'd'.

D

E

F

G

6. Make your first stitch by putting the needle into the centre loop. Observe how the cord forms a loop above this – you will be bringing the needle up through this loop to form the first stitch (**D**). It can help to rearrange your hold on the work so that your thumb now covers this stitch, and the centre loop is obvious. This can make it easier to put your needle into the right place on the next stitch.

7. Make 8 blanket stitches around the centre loop working into the original starting loop for each stitch (**E**). This completes Round 1. Simple looping and looping round a core work well with eight starting stitches; in stitches you will encounter later in the book, we will use different starting numbers.

8. The round start will look like a flower with eight petals (**F**), and it can help to think in terms of 'petals' rather than 'loops' on the next round, as you start increasing. Your work will develop in a spiral; if desired, add a stitch marker to help you identify the start of each round as you come to it. In Round 2 we will be increasing into every stitch by working twice into the same loop of the round beneath.

9. Continue as you have been doing, and make a blanket stitch/simple loop into the top of the next 'petal'. Immediately, make a second stitch into the same space. You now have 2 stitches where previously you had 1. Move to the next petal and do the same thing. At the end of this round your 8 stitches will have become 16 (**G**).

Tip

Sizing your loops: You can make these loops very tight and small, or you can make them very large and open. For your first experiments, I suggest that you aim for something you can comfortably pull the needle through but without being too open. This helps the work develop a definite structure very early on, making it easier to work neatly and evenly.

Working a round start using ready-made yarn

The principle is the same as working with cordage, but you won't have that convenient starting loop to pull the end through. For this example, we will assume you are using a plant-fibre yarn that will not felt.

1. Cut a piece of yarn measuring about two arms' lengths, and thread one end onto a needle.

2. Bring the tail around so that you have a loop with the working end coming out of the top of it (**A**), as with the cordage version on p. 49. You will use this tail later to pull the starting loop tight, and then weave in the end neatly. Alternatively, start with a slip knot and work into the loop, drawing up the loop to close the circle at the end of the first round.

3. Work Steps 5, 6 and 7 of the round start using cord-as-you-go (**B**, **C**, **D**).
   When you need to join in new yarn, you have two main options. You could use a Russian join but an overlapped or 'lazy' join is more in keeping with these very early structures and works particularly well if the loops are worked reasonably snugly (see Joining in new yarn, p. 26).

A

B

C

D

4. Lay the new yarn along the top of the circle and work over it for a few stitches with the last of your old yarn (**E**). In this example, two colours are used for clarity.

5. When you have caught the new yarn into place, thread it onto the needle and lay the final tail of the old yarn along your work. Work over the old yarn until it runs out. Continue with the new yarn.

Above: Hairnet made using simple looping in flax and inspired by headwear seen on prehistoric figurines

Working a flat circle

Creating a flat circle in nalbinding uses the same principle as working a beret or granny square in knitting or crochet. After the second round, you will start leaving more spaces between increases. Whenever you start running short of cord, pause and make more onto the live end of the cordage. This way, your work will be completely seamless, and there will be no need to join new lengths of yarn using knots.

Abbreviations

Inc: work 2 stitches into 1 loop

Work x plain: work 1 stitch into each of the next x loops

Rep *-*: Repeat instructions between asterisks all the way around

Round 3: *Inc, work 1 plain*, rep *-*. This means that you will increase into the first loop (work 2 stitches into 1 'petal'), then work 1 stitch into the second loop, and repeat these two steps all the way around. Your 16 stitches have now become 24.

Round 4: *Inc, work 2 plain*, rep*-*. 32 stitches.

Round 5: *Inc, work 3 plain*, rep*-*. 40 stitches.

To continue working a flat disc, work more rounds with one additional plain stitch in each increase set (i.e., Round 6 would read *Inc, work 4 plain*). Because your work spirals around itself, there shouldn't be any 'steps' where the next round starts.

If you want to start a three-dimensional shape, such as a bag or hat, I suggest working a round without increases after Round 5. This lets you see how things are looping, and will start to create a very gentle curve from the flat base.

To continue a curved form, decide whether you need to increase further, or whether working in the round, one stitch into each loop, will give the right effect. Your work will not suddenly turn a right angle when you work plain; rather it will curve up gradually and will almost always end up a little wider than the flat base. You can also put in increases intuitively as needed if a curved shape needs to become just a little wider.

These simple looping forms are useful for making bags, hair coverings and things like strainers. Historically, they may have been used as nets, but we also know that true netting using the same sheet bend knot we use in hand-made nets today can be traced back over 10,000 years, so it's likely that nets needed for larger, potentially wriggly contents were made in the same way as traditional fishing nets.

Simple looping can be used decoratively too; nalbound stitches are seen as structural elements and as applied decoration on Bronze Age woollen clothing. Several surviving garments from the Northern European Bronze Age (1700–500 BCE) show embroidery based on looped stitches or sections of looping used to join heavy fabrics together.

Above: A round start worked in loop-and-twist stitch

Left: Changing twist direction in a jar cover

Tip

Direction of twist: you will see differences in the direction of twist in your stitches depending on whether you are working right- or left-handed, or putting the needle through the foundation loop from the front or from the back. Changing twist direction in an otherwise simple project such as the jar cover pictured can add a lot of interest for no extra effort.

String bag in simple looping

This project is inspired by stitches found on Neolithic archaeological sites, including this 5,000-year-old example of corded oak bast from Switzerland. We are going to use the same technique to make a practical bag, but for this project we will use easily available raffia. This can be obtained in small amounts in many brightly dyed colours from craft suppliers, but for the most cost-effective resource, look at floristry suppliers, where hanks of unbleached raffia can be bought by the kilo.

DIFFICULTY: Intermediate, but only because making the cordage will add time to the work

Above: Horgen Culture (3500–2850 BCE), Feldmeilen, Switzerland. ©Kantonsarchäologie Zürich, Photographer: Martin Bachmann

You will need:

- Raffia (45g for my example)

- A needle large enough to thread your cordage onto

To begin

1. Raffia needs to be dampened before use for the neatest results. Take a handful and dip it in water, then drain and let it sit for half an hour or so (**A**). This makes the slightly stiff fibres pliable and much easier to work. There is no need to over soak – too much water makes dry plant fibres swell up, and this can lead to shrinkage when it dries, making your cordage loose. It's a good idea to experiment a little to see how much dampening gives you the best results.

   Raffia tends to come in fairly uniform strips, but you will get much nicer cordage if you split each strip down into sections a couple of millimetres wide before starting your cord. You don't need to do the whole batch at once; usually it is convenient to separate three or four strips into smaller sections, and then turn those into cordage. This lets you add in new material frequently and evenly for neat string.

2. Following the cordage instructions (see Making cord, p. 46), make a piece of cord one or two arms' lengths, leaving the working end available to add more fibre to as needed (**B**). The beauty of a cord-as-you-go project is that your work will have no knots or joins in it – just smooth, continuous cordage. If you do get any ends that stick out and annoy you, these can be clipped off.

3. Starting with 8 loops, work a flat circle (see Working a flat circle, p. 52) until the base of your bag is as wide as you want it (**C**). It may help to mark the start of the round with a stitch marker. Add to your cordage as necessary.

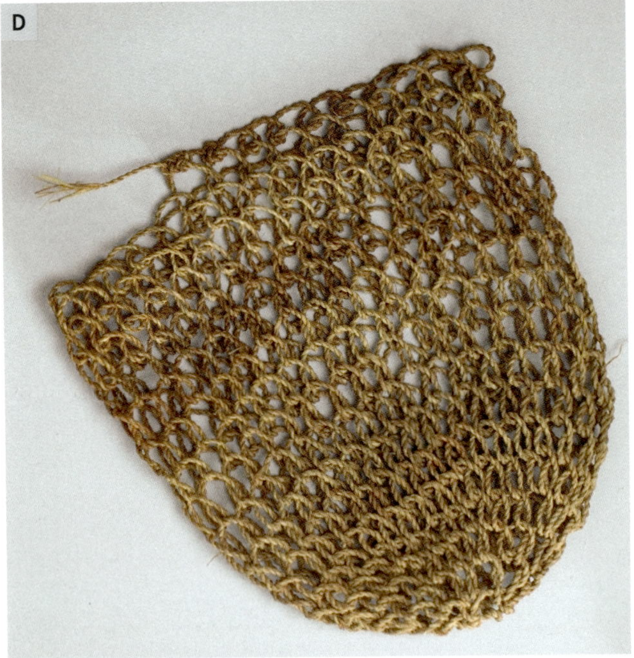

4. Once the base is complete, work 1 stitch into each loop in spirals until your bag is as big as you want it (**D**). It is normal for a bag to look a little smaller and more crumpled during working than it will at the end, but the loops will settle during finishing.

5. When you are nearly done, allow your cordage to taper off a little and make 2 or 3 tight stitches close together to secure the end.

6. Make a length of cord to use as a drawstring and thread it through the top loops of the bag.

7. Dampen the whole thing and stretch it over something approximately the right size. This might be a bowl, a ball or a rolled-up towel. Be inventive! Pull firmly on the bag to settle the loops into place, and check whether there are any large or small loops that can be gently adjusted to a more uniform size at this stage. Allow the bag to dry completely (**E**).

Looping around a core (Tybrind Vig stitch)

This variation is named for a series of fragments from a waterlogged Danish Mesolithic site at Tybrind Vig, and has only one technical difference from simple looping: it uses a passive secondary yarn carried along the work as it develops to add extra structure. This stops the work stretching along the path of the core yarn.

If you have just tried the round start exercise using a cut yarn and have joined in by laying the new yarn along the work, you have already worked a little of this stitch!

Above: A selection of grass baskets that have been looped around a core

Originally, this start would also have been made using a cord-as-you-go technique, but today we can make use of the availability of large balls of twine to speed things up. This does mean that you need to join in new lengths of cord periodically, but this stitch lends itself to that very well, which makes it a great stitch to use with stiffer plant-fibre string. If worked in a heavy material, your end result will be similar in form to a basket; if worked in something softer and more flexible, it creates robust fabrics for phone cases, dice bags or amulet pouches.

For the Tybrind Vig-stitch shopping basket project, you will use a slightly modified start, setting up with an oval rather than a round base. The phone case and dice bag projects use soft, colourful yarn, highlighting how different effects can be achieved based entirely on yarn choice.

It is important to remember that your core thread is passive. You work over it with each stitch, but the core thread does not move in the process. You can add new working or core thread as needed by laying the new material along the existing core and working over it for a few stitches.

Shopping basket

This robust shopper or storage bag uses thick sisal twine and a stitch that we can trace right back into the Mesolithic, about 6,500 years ago. I've chosen a thick 3mm twine that works up quickly, but you can use thinner string too – it will just take a little longer.

DIFFICULTY: Simple

You will need:

- Thick sisal twine
- A needle large enough to thread your cordage onto
- A piece of string or a stitch marker

Abbreviations

Inc: work 2 stitches into 1 loop
Work x plain: work 1 stitch into each of the next x loops
Rep *-*: Repeat instructions between asterisks all the way around

1. You are going to begin with an oval start and introduce the core twine right from the beginning. The core thread will carry through the whole project, so it's a good plan to wind off a manageable ball from your main stock of twine right from the start (**A**). If it tries to unwind as you work, wrapping an elastic band around it can help. Leave about two arms' lengths free to start the looping with.

2. Work simple loops over the core thread until you have several loops (**B**). In this example, I have made 16 loops. This makes half the set-up round.

Tips

- If the twine frays a little at the end, a scrap of tape can control it and act as a needle, but you will be changing lengths of twine regularly so I recommend using a large-eyed needle.

- Smooth any escaping fibres back into place as you work by giving the end a little twist in the direction it was originally spun. This will quickly become automatic.

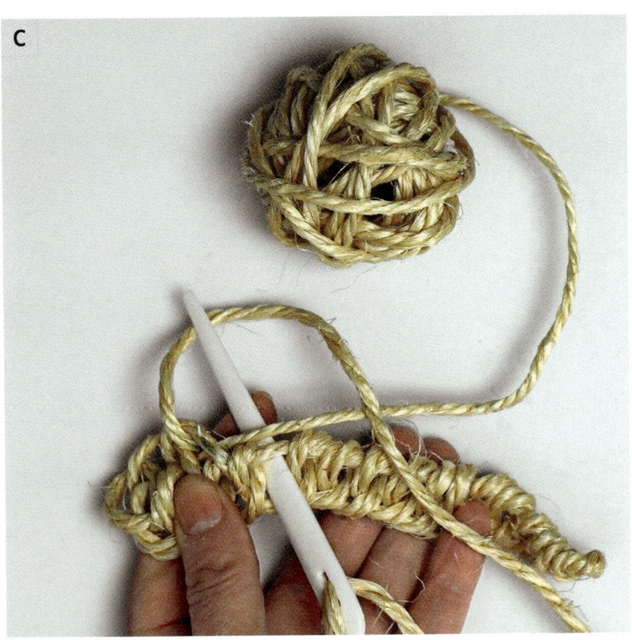

3. Bend the work around so that the core thread runs above the previous core (**C**). This means that for the second half of the set-up round you will work over both the current core thread and the one in the first half of the round, making your new stitches in the gaps between the existing ones. This makes a solid starting round and puts all the loops in the same direction for working the rest of the basket in the round.

4. To increase the base to form a flat oval, you need to add stitches on the next round. Identify 4 points, 2 at each end of the oval (**D**) and mark them with a piece of string or a marker. You are going to work twice into each of these stitches.

> Round 1: *Inc, work plain to the next marked stitch, inc*, rep *-* once more.

If you are using thick string, you may only need to repeat Round 1 once or twice more to reach a good size for your bag or basket base.

You will need to add new twine at some point. To do this, cut a new length that you can comfortably manage (try two arms' lengths to start with and as you get more confident, you can try using a little more) and lay it next to the core thread. Work over it with the existing twine for a few stitches until only a few centimetres is left, then swap the new thread for the old. Lay the tail end of the old thread next to the core and carry on with the new thread. This slight extra thickness will barely be noticeable once the project is finished and this is a fast and easy way to add more thread when using chunky material.

5. Now that the base is established, all the stitches will be worked as standard looping over a core. Don't worry if the work twists at this point (**E**) – it will settle as you progress. You can correct this before starting the sides by dampening the piece then allowing it to dry flat under a weight.

6. Once the base is complete and flattened (if desired), work 1 round without any increases before starting the sides (**F**).

7. Now for the body:
   Round 1: Inc 4 times as evenly as possible around.
   Round 2: Work plain (**G**).

   Repeat these 2 rounds until the bag is the desired size. I suggest shifting the position of your increases each time to give a smooth finish to the basket.

Tip

At the end of each half round check that your core thread is neither too tight nor too loose, as this will affect how flat your work lies. It can be useful to pull on it slightly to draw it in a little, then stretch the edge of the work with your hands to settle it back to the desired size. This can allow you to make subtle changes to the basket diameter if needed.

8. If you want to make a handle, this is easily worked in looping around a core stitch. At the point where you want to place the handle, stop linking to the row below and make a chain long enough to form the handle (**H**). Reattach the work and continue the round. To make sure the second handle matches the first, take note of how many stitches you used to make it, and pay attention to where you locate the second handle on the other side of the work. You may not need to count stitches exactly to find the start and end point, but do consider the overall size of the loop and where you should reattach it. You may want to work another round or 2 over this in fine yarn to make a more substantial handle, but in the heavy cord used here, 1 round is sufficient.

9. Finish off by making a few tighter stitches, then weave the ends of the looping yarn and then the core yarn into the rows below to hide them. Clip off any ends, then lightly dampen the basket and pat it into shape before allowing it to dry.

PROJECT 4

Phone case

DIFFICULTY: Simple
RECOMMENDED STITCH: Looping around a core
JOINING METHOD: Overlapped join

You will need:

- Approximately 25g/45m (148ft) of bright craft cotton. Choose something that is not too thin. Variegated or ombre yarn can be very useful, as you can clearly see your stitches as you work. My sample used 24g aran-weight dishcloth cotton.

- A needle

A

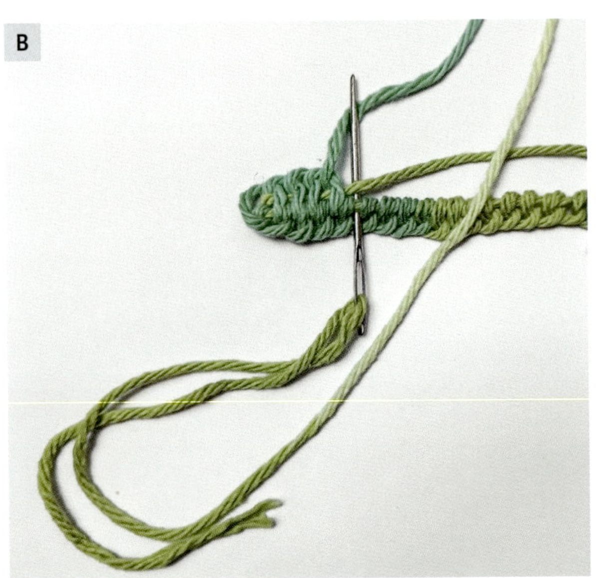

B

1. Work a foundation row as wide as your intended case, allowing an extra stitch or two for tightening up a little after the set-up row (**A**).

2. Bend the core thread around so that you can work back along the first row to give a solid foundation (**B**).

3. For the body, work in spirals from the foundation row upwards, overlapping new yarn in as needed (**C**).

4. When the case is tall enough, finish by working several very tight stitches to taper the edge, then weave in any ends. Rinse through and pat to shape before allowing to dry.

Dice bag

DIFFICULTY: Simple
RECOMMENDED STITCH: Looping around a core
JOINING METHOD: Overlapped join

You will need:

- Approximately 25g/45m (148ft) of bright craft cotton. Choose something that is not too thin. Variegated or ombre yarn can be very useful, as you can clearly see your stitches as you work. My sample used 24g aran-weight dishcloth cotton.

- A needle

1. Make a round start using looping over a core stitch (**A**).

2. Once your base is as wide as you want your bag to be, work the body in rounds without any increases until the bag is the size you want.

3. Finish as for the phone case and add a drawstring to the top.

Cross-knit looping (Coptic stitch, Tarim stitch)

Of all nalbinding stitches, this one has caused the most confusion, because it really does look like knitting at first glance. It even has a purl as well as a knit side.

In **A** and **B**, the top few rows have been worked with knitting needles, twisting each stitch by working into the back loop. The lower few rows have been nalbound. With a little attention to the path the yarn takes, the two can be almost indistinguishable, and it is only by determining in which direction a piece was worked (usually by closely examining any increases or decreases) that some archaeological finds can be conclusively labelled as knit or nalbound. It is highly likely that there are still collections containing misidentified examples.

A remarkable 15x17cm textile fragment found at Dura-Europos is so like knitting, with plain and purl sections, that scholars only recently confirmed it as nalbinding. It is a patterned section of a sock dating from third-century Syria, and must have looked very luxurious when worn.

It does not appear to be made in varied colours, so relies on the effect of the textured stitches to make the pattern visible, much as we see in Aran sweaters today, where clever use of plain and purl knitting creates complex patterns.

A remarkable number of socks survive from the late Roman period in Egypt and neighbouring regions. They were designed to be worn with sandals, and can be plain

or make use of several distinct stitches. Many have a split-toe construction, and the ones sized for children are frequently worked in cheerful stripes and a stitch that looks very much like knitting at first glance. This stitch, properly called cross-knit looping, is also known as Coptic stitch. It is also sometimes named Tarim stitch after the hats found with the Tarim Basin mummies, although they were not worked in this stitch at all. However, stitch names tend to stick regardless of how they come about, and you will hear many stitches called by various names.

Compared to the simple looping and looping around a core stitch we studied in the last chapter, which lend themselves to cord-as-you-go construction and the use of plant fibres, cross-knit looping is frequently found worked in wool, and a closer look at those stripey Egyptian socks may give us some insights into why.

Before industrialisation allowed for rapid and cost-effective production, producing yarn was time consuming and therefore valuable and not something to be wasted. Weaving on early looms frequently resulted in short, leftover lengths of warp threads (thrums) after the cloth was cut off the weights or beams. These are often long enough to be useful for techniques like nalbinding.

Fabrics, leather and other materials are likely to have been coloured with ochres or stained with plants from very early in prehistory, but true dyes take time to develop. The oldest known example of dyed cotton is a 6,000-year-old fragment from Peru coloured with indigo. Another example, from Israel, is a 3,800-year-old Bronze Age piece of fabric, which has a woollen weft dyed scarlet with kermes (a dye derived from insects native to the Mediterranean, suggesting extensive trade networks). Dyed yarn becomes increasingly common in Europe during the Iron Age, with complex dyeing and mordanting techniques allowing for a range of stable, light-fast colours.

By the Coptic period in Egypt (roughly the third to ninth centuries CE), dye technology was well advanced, and a range of colours appeared frequently, including blue from woad or indigo, yellow from a wide range of plants including safflower (*Carthamus tinctorius*) or weld (*Reseda luteola* – more common in Europe) and red from the roots of the madder plant (*Rubia tinctorum*) or from insect dyes. It is not hard to imagine that relatively short lengths of valuable, brightly dyed yarn left over from larger weaving or braiding projects were repurposed for small projects such as children's socks. With time, it may be that yarn was spun specifically for socks, but the short working lengths continued to lend themselves well to stripes, especially in children's garments.

Above: **Yarns dyed with woad, weld and madder – dyes that have been widely used since late prehistory**

Working cross-knit looping

Projects such as socks can be started from a round start (see simple looping, p. 44) and flat pieces from a chain-stitch start. Cross-knit looping is a needle-tensioned stitch, and so can be worked extremely densely if desired, as well as more airily. Like knitting, this stitch tends to curl towards the stockinette side.

A chain stitch, or finger-crochet chain is a useful foundation for cross-knit looping.

1. Start the chain by making a slip knot (**A**).

2. Pull a new loop through the previous one using your fingers until your chain is the desired length (**B**).

3. Start the cross-knit looping by working through the loops on whichever side of the chain is most convenient. Insert the needle into the foundation row from the front and bring it up to the left, making a little cross of the threads below (**C**).

4. Pull the yarn through and bring your needle to the right, ready to make the next stitch.

Working flat

Most nalbinding is easiest when worked in the round, but working this stitch flat is quite straightforward. You might notice that your stitches cross in opposite directions on RS/WS rows; this is perfectly normal if using the same working motions on each row. It can be worked in a way that keeps the loops crossing in one direction, although this requires a slightly different yarn path in the stitches going in each direction. It is up to you whether you find this a necessary refinement or not.

To work garter-stitch rows: at the end of each row, make 1 simple loop as a turning stitch then just flip the work over so you are working on the opposite side. This will give the characteristic ribbed garter stitch (**A**).

To work flat rows using the same stitch path for a stockinette fabric: at the end of a row, make a turning stitch. As you work back along the row pay particular attention to how your needle crosses the loop of yarn to make it mimic the preceding row (**B**). Some people find it easiest to turn the work upside down for this row; others work it left-handed.

You can also work flat rows without modifying the path of the stitch. The 'V' shapes created by each stitch on the stockinette side will look slightly different in alternating rows, but this may be fine in certain projects. Try both methods and see which you like best!

Increases and decreases

In most instances, the simplest way to create and increase in cross-knit looping is to work a simple loop increase (see Working a flat circle, p. 52).

Decreases can be made by either skipping a stitch, which may result in a small eyelet forming, or by picking up two stitches and working them together (**C**).

Festival socks

For these two projects, I have taken inspiration from the many examples of child-sized Coptic socks and used short sections of brightly coloured yarn (a great stash buster) to make exuberant and playful socks, just right for cosying up in the evening at a festival camp, or for use as slipper socks. Whether you work a round toe or two-toed socks is up to you. The two versions of the project illustrate how distinctive the socks can look with different toe treatments.

You could plan these in regular, even stripes with a definite colour scheme, or go for a more pick-and-mix approach, using an arm's length of yarn chosen at random every time. I've even used inherited collections of tapestry wool for this type of project, each skein being an ideal length to divide into two, one part for each sock.

The tendency of this stitch to curl is used to advantage here to create a soft roll top at the ankle.

Tips

- Make both socks at the same time: work an arm's length or two on one, then the same on the other. Although a general recipe for a sock worked in this stitch is given below, the exact number of stitches and rows will vary according to the thickness of your yarn and the tension you use. Making two at a time allows you to easily remember the shaping you have used. If you want even stripes and are working with scraps of yarn, this method is also the best way to make sure you use the same amount on each sock.

- I used a felted join in the sample, which does result in a blending of shades at the join. If you find this method a little too messy, you can fold the ends back on themselves for a cleaner shade transition (see Joining in new yarn, p. 26).

Troubleshooting

Try on the socks regularly as you work, if possible: to avoid the ankle area being too loose, you will need to make the instep long enough before starting the heel flap. The grey striped sock pictured has two problem areas. The instep was a little short, resulting in a slightly longer heel flap than was ideal, and this resulted in a loose, baggy ankle section. Trying it on regularly would have made this clear, allowing for early corrections to be made.

Conversely, it can be easy to make the ankle area a little too tight, making it hard to pull the socks on. If you think this is starting to happen as you work up the ankle area, rather than working the cuff in the round, work it flat with a split at the front. You can always add a string to tie the top shut – a feature seen on some early socks.

This sock was abandoned before finishing due to problems with fit.

Children's two-toed Coptic sock

This split-toe option is inspired by a surviving sock in the collection at Manchester Museum, and takes its row counts and colour choices from that. I used around 70g of aran-weight yarn for the larger sample pictured. If you use a lighter yarn, you will need more stitches. Interestingly, two sample pairs made to essentially the same pattern with similar yarn came out at different sizes. This was due partly to needle size and partly to tension – I pulled the stitches tighter on the smaller pair. This reinforces the advisability of making both socks in a pair at once!

DIFFICULTY: Intermediate

You will need:

- Approximately 70g/100m (328ft) of aran-weight yarn

- A needle

Above: **Child's Coptic sock.** © Manchester Museum, The University of Manchester. Photographer: Michael Pollard

1. Start by making two toe cups: one will take the big toe, or the big and second toe and the second will take the remaining smaller toes.

   A. For the smaller toe cup, make a round start of 12 stitches using simple looping.
   > **Round 1:** Switch to cross-knit looping and work 12 stitches plain. Place a stitch marker to help identify where the rounds start from here.
   > **Round 2:** Work 12 stitches plain, increase by making a simple loop. 13 stitches.
   > **Round 3:** Work 13 stitches plain, increase as before. 14 stitches.
   > **Rounds 4–10:** Work 14 stitches plain.

   This completes the smaller toe cup.

2. **B.** For the larger toe cup, make a round start of 12 stitches using simple looping.
   > **Rounds 1–3:** Work as for Rounds 1–3 of smaller toe cup. 14 stitches.
   > **Round 4:** Work 14 stitches plain, increase as before. 15 stitches.
   > **Round 5:** Work 15 stitches, increase as before. 16 stitches.
   > **Rounds 6–10:** Work 16 stitches plain.

   This completes the larger toe cup.

> **Tip**
> You might consider making this larger toe cup one round shorter – many people have much shorter small toes than big toe.

3. Make the second set to match.

4. Now to join the toe cups: place them side by side with the increases facing outwards then switch to your second colour (blue in **C**) and work round both cups to join them together. You will probably lose two stitches where the cups meet, so expect to end up with 28 stitches at the end of this round. Any small gaps where the toe cups meet and any tails of yarn from the toe cups can be darned in before finishing.

5. Work 6 rounds in your second colour, increasing 1 stitch on the final round on the underside of the foot. 29 stitches.

6. Work 4 rounds in your first colour, increasing 1 stitch on the final round on the underside of the foot. 30 stitches.

7. Work 6 rounds in your third colour (I used yellow), increasing as before. 31 stitches.

8. Work 4 rounds in your first colour, increasing as before. 32 stitches.

9. Work 1 round in your third colour.

10. For the heel flap, use your second colour and start at the outer edge of a toe cup, working 14 stitches (or as needed to meet the other edge of the toes).

11. Work 12 rows flat over these 14 stitches, remembering to add one simple loop at the end of each row to allow you to turn the work.

12. Work 2 rows flat, leaving off the extra stitch at the end of the row. This will narrow the work by 1 stitch each time (D). 12 stitches. Weave in the end of the yarn.

13. To start bringing the heel up, join your third colour at one side of the heel flap and work round the 3 sides of the sole. You should have approximately 36 stitches.

Above: **The sock in progress**

D

14. Switch to your first colour, and picking up the corresponding coloured purl loops behind the yellow stripe at the edge of the instep every time you reach it, work back and forth to start shaping the heel (**E**). You may want to work the 2 stitches on the rear corner of the sole flap together in Rows 1 and 2 to encourage a good shape. This will leave you with 32 stitches.

Tip
Pay attention to your tension when working flat. It is easy to make this area tighter than you intend compared to when working in the round, which is fine if you know you are doing it and can check it is not going to distort the fit.

15. Work 6 rows using your first colour.

16. Work 10 rows using your second colour. This should bring you up to the top of the instep. The remainder of the sock is worked in the round.

17. Heading up to the ankle, work 3 rounds using your first colour.

18. Work 10 rounds using your third colour.

19. Work 2 rounds using your first colour.

E

F

20. Finish by weaving in any ends, then turn the socks inside out and check for gaps between the toe cups. Darn in a stitch there if needed (**F**).

21. Wash the socks gently and pat them into shape.

Then you simply have to decide who they will fit! The nice thing about these child-sized socks is that they don't take a huge amount of time, meaning you can plan adjustments in stitch count or tension if you find you need a second try to fit the intended recipient (**G**).

G

Festival sock with round toe

The sample pictured is an adult UK size 6. You will need a few more stitches and rows for bigger sizes.

DIFFICULTY: Intermediate
JOINING METHOD: Felted or Russian

You will need:

● Aran-weight yarn. The pictured version was worked to give a gauge of approximately 22 stitches per 10cm, and used around 130g/185m (607ft) of yarn

● A needle

Abbreviations

Inc: work 2 stitches into 1 stitch

Work x plain: work 1 stitch into each of the next x stitches

Rep *-*: Repeat instructions between asterisks all the way around

1. Start with the toe, with a round start of 8 stitches.
   Round 1: Inc in each stitch around. 16 stitches.
   Round 2: *Inc, work 1 plain*, rep *-*. 24 stitches.
   Round 3: Work plain.
   Round 4: *Inc, work 2 plain*, rep *-*. 32 stitches.
   Round 5: Work plain.
   Round 6: *Inc, work 3 plain*, rep *-*. 40 stitches.
   Round 7: Work plain.
   Round 8: *Inc, work 4 plain*, rep *-*. 48 stitches.
   Round 9: Work plain.

A

B

2. Try the sock toe on. It should fully cover your toes. If you need a wider sock, work 1 more increase round (*inc, work 5 plain*, rep *-*, 56 stitches) and try on again.

3. Moving to the instep, work plain until the sock reaches the point where your leg joins the foot. If you have high arches you may need to add a couple of increases as you near this point to allow extra room. The pictured sample (A) took 40 rounds to reach this point.

4. The heel flap is worked in approximately 21 flat rounds of 16 stitches and needs to be wide enough to cover the underside of your heel. If your sock is wider than this sample, you might need 2 more stitches. See notes on working flat (p.33) for tips on getting a neat turn.

5. Work 1 round flat, decreasing 1 stitch at each end. This gives a neater finish when you start the heel. 14 stitches.

6. To begin the heel, start working back and forth around the edge of the heel flap, picking up stitches

from the instep as you reach them. You can either continue working from the end of the heel along the nearest side of the heel flap or, as in B, join new yarn (white in the sample pictured) at the start of the flap and work round all 3 sides. Aim to pick up around 17 stitches on each side. With the 14 stitches at the back of the heel this will add up to the same number of stitches you had at the instep (48). If you worked a wider sock or longer heel flap pick up more stitches as needed. You may need to estimate where to put the needle to make even stitches if your turns are not clear but if the final count is even on both sides, it will be fine.

7. When you reach the instep, put your needle through the nearest loop to anchor your work as you turn (C).

8. Continue to work back and forth in rows around the ankle, picking up instep stitches as you reach them until you are nearly at the top of the sock. Try the sock on periodically and check that you have a comfortable fit. If the sock seems tight, an increase or two can be made, but it's more common to find the sock a little loose if you have picked up more stitches than you started with. In this case, look at where

decreases will be the most use and put them in strategically. Often, this will be at the 'corner' where the heel flap turns.

9. You have a choice to make as you near the top of the instep. If you have plenty of room for your foot and ankle, you can continue picking up instep stitches right to the top of the sock. However, if you need a little more width for your ankle, stop working flat while there is still a centimetre or two to go, and switch to working in the round, picking up the remaining instep stitches as you go. This will give a wider cuff section. If the fit is good, you can continue working flat and picking up instep stitches until they are all used up, then either work flat for the whole cuff to give a split at the front (**D**), or work in the round for a tubular sock style cuff.

10. When your sock is long enough, you can secure the remaining tail of yarn. The nature of this stitch means that the top edge will roll outwards a little. If you worked a split cuff, you might consider adding a drawstring and maybe tassels for tying the top closed.

11. Rinse the finished socks through and pat them into shape before allowing them to dry. This evens out stitches and makes everything much more regular. If the socks are slightly big, a gentle fulling will shrink suitable wools down to size.

C

D

York stitch (also called Coppergate stitch, Jorvik stitch)

The Coppergate sock is the only surviving complete piece of nalbinding found in Britain, and as it is a single sock may be empirical proof that the odd-sock monster has inhabited these shores for over 1,000 years. Worked in a very fine stitch at 36 rows to 10cm, this can be scaled up to make no-nonsense, easily worked garments.

The Coppergate site in York produced a wide range of organic archaeological remains and offered a unique insight into life in tenth-century

Above: **Coppergate Sock.**
© York Archaeology

northern England during what is often loosely called the Viking Age (Walton 1989). Because no other complete piece of nalbinding is known from Britain, it is unclear whether this sock was made locally, or travelled to Jorvik (the early medieval name for York) on the foot of a Scandinavian trader. Consequently, we don't know whether it represents a local tradition in widespread contemporary use, or if it's a more exotic import, especially as there don't appear to be any other examples from Europe that used exactly this stitch.

Analysis of the yarn showed that the wool could have originated anywhere in England, Denmark or Ireland. Theories abound as to its origins: it could be a local stitch variant, or perhaps someone misremembered a similar stitch learnt elsewhere. In a frequently unsettled period, crafts, trade and art could play an important stabilising role by linking populations in different areas, and it's tempting to imagine that the maker of these socks had a life story that included travel between northern Europe and northern Britain, and a need to make practical clothing for themselves or a family member. The last row of the ankle-high sock was worked in madder-dyed yarn; madder was a plant dye used commercially in Jorvik to produce rich orangey-red fabrics that were extremely popular at the time.

Working York stitch

Hansen's notation: UU/OOO F2

When first viewed, York stitch can look confusing, especially if you are trying it after simple looping or cross-knit looping, but it's one of the easiest stitches to learn and doesn't need to be tensioned over the thumb. You can work this very tightly in fine yarn for a smooth, dense fabric like the original sock, or use heavier yarn and leave it a little looser for thick, warm garments.

Above: **A chain of York stitch**

It might be helpful to visualise this stitch as a form of blanket stitch that also picks up the previous two stitches. It is very dense and elastic, and the F2 connection means that each row overlaps the one before by half. Like most nalbinding, it doesn't easily run or unravel if cut or torn, making it an excellent choice for socks.

The finished fabric does tend to curl. Although this doesn't make any real difference when the garment is being worn, it can make working from a starting chain annoying, especially if you are new to nalbinding. I recommend trying it first either from a round start, or by building on a foundation worked onto something else, as in the sock toppers project in this chapter. It is denser than simple looping or cross-knit looping, so bear that in mind if combining different stitches in one project.

Above: **The F2 connection in York stitch**

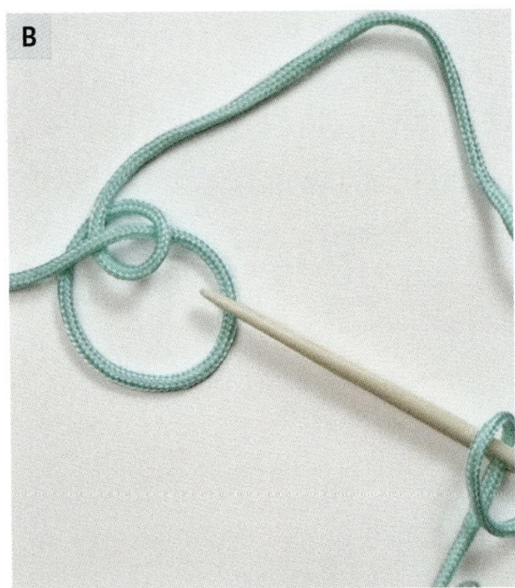

A round start in York stitch

A round start in York stitch is only a little different to the one you've already encountered in simple looping, and this is a useful start to practise if you aspire to making a full-scale replica of the Coppergate sock.

1. Start by making a loop (**A**).

2. Work a simple loop into it (**B**).

3. In the second stitch, also come up through the last loop as well as the central loop (**C**). This is sometimes called half York stitch and can be a useful variation in very thick yarn.

4. In the third stitch, come up through both the previous loops (**D**). You are now working in York stitch.

5. Continue to work stitches by putting the needle into the centre of the loop, then up through 2 loops of the recently formed stitches. A round start in this stitch is usually best with around 12 or 13 stitches (**E**). Compare this to the round start in simple looping that typically starts with just 8 stitches. York stitch is a much denser stitch.

6. After this start the formula is the same as it was for simple looping or looping around a core.

7. Increases are made by working an additional stitch into the same hole, again picking up the 2 previous loops. In the second round, increase into every stitch to double the number of stitches (**F**).

Continue increasing as you did with the round start in simple looping:
> **Round 3:** Work 1 plain, increase into the next stitch, repeat from * to * around.
> **Round 4:** Work 2 plain, increase into the next stitch, repeat from * to * around.

Continue in this way, leaving an additional stitch between increases in each round until the starting disc is as wide as you wish.

For curved shapes such as sock toes it is a good idea to work an occasional plain round so you can assess whether the toe cup is wide enough.

E

F

Decreases are made most simply by skipping a hole or working two loops together.

- The heel section of the Coppergate sock was worn through and patched during its lifetime, so it's now quite hard to be sure exactly what pattern was used for the heel beyond being able to see some wedges of shaping in the damaged areas.

Right: Several heel options are provided in *Part four: Socks* if you decide to try your hand at a reconstruction or a sock inspired by this, such as the one pictured here

Sock toppers

Over the past 25 years, I've taught many early medieval re-enactors how to use York stitch to make socks inspired by the Coppergate find. Understandably, a whole pair of socks in a fine gauge is quite a daunting project for a first-time nalbinder, and I sometimes suggested a fast warm-up version that allowed them to practise the stitch while still ending up with something they could wear with historical costuming if they didn't mind the hidden areas being a little anachronistic. This same approach allows the modern crafter to take advantage of a single skein of beautiful yarn to make statement sock toppers to wear with boots. The lovely thing about this project is that it requires no shaping, so you can concentrate on getting used to working the stitch without any technical challenges.

DIFFICULTY: Simple

You'll need:

- A pair of comfortable socks a little shorter than the intended boots

- A sharp needle for the first round

- A nalbinding needle that suits the yarn

- A skein of yarn (a 50g skein is usually more than enough for a good deep pair of sock toppers). As these are for socks, you may wish to choose something easily laundered, but bear in mind a felted join may not work well on this. See the section on joining yarn for ideas.

To begin

Start by putting on the socks and checking how much they stretch around your leg at the cuff end. You'll need to make sure the starting row isn't too tight as you work. If it helps, consider putting the cuff of the sock over a piece of cardboard of approximately the right size as you work the first round.

Using a sharp needle and your chosen yarn, work the
first round of York stitch around the top of each sock.
If you are using a very thick yarn, you may want to do a
foundation row of blanket stitch in something thinner; this
will give you clear loops through which to work the first
thicker layer of yarn.

1. Make a simple loop into the top of the sock (a blanket
   stitch) (**A**). The second stitch can pick up the previous
   stitch (half York stitch). From here on in there will be
   enough stitches on the sock to work in York stitch.

2. Pierce the edge of the sock with each stitch, then pick
   up 2 of the previous stitches as you pull the new loop
   through (**B**). Try the sock on at the end of this round
   to be sure it stretches over your ankle.

   Remember not to pull too tightly; the sock must be
   able to stretch to fit your leg later and York stitch pulls
   in a little as you start working it. The exact number of
   stitches you make will depend on your yarn. Expect
   to make approximately 120 stitches if you are using a
   sock-weight yarn, and perhaps 100 if using DK-weight
   if you want a dense finish like the Coppergate sock
   (**C**). For an airier finish, you can work this stitch much
   more loosely and you will need far fewer starting
   stitches.

3. Work around in spirals until the sock topper is as long as you want it to be. I recommend working any sock project as a matched pair, using one length of yarn on each sock in turn. This helps ensure similar tension on both as well as making the most out of stripes of hand-spun or hand-painted yarn. Try on the socks periodically and, if necessary, make an occasional increase or decrease to suit the effect you want (**D**).

4. To finish the sock toppers once they are long enough, weave in any ends then gently hand wash the socks and lay them to dry, patting the tops into shape. It's normal for there to be a little bit of twist at the top; this is a feature of this stitch (**E**). Try them on with your favourite boots!

PART THREE:
THUMB-TENSIONED STITCHES

The medieval period in Europe reached its peak towards the end of the thirteenth century, and this rapidly changing world introduced new textile techniques. Knitting became widely used for socks, caps and mittens, whereas they had previously been made either from cut and sewn cloth or by methods such as nalbinding or sprang.

Nalbinding, however, remained a living tradition in many areas, and several examples of garments associated with saints or clergy are preserved in ecclesiastic collections. These garments also represent everyday items that would have been familiar to the secular population. Other surviving garments are the result of lucky preservation, like the Oslo mitten pictured overleaf, which was found under a wooden floor where it had lain forgotten since its loss some 900 years ago.

Nalbound mittens appear to have been commonly made from the medieval period onwards, and they are well represented in the archaeological and historical record. While these still make an ideal project today, the stitches recorded in these mittens are extremely versatile, lending themselves well to hats, bags and even socks.

Earlier in this book, we looked at stitches that are tensioned on the needle or drawn up freehand to the required size. This section covers stitches that all rely

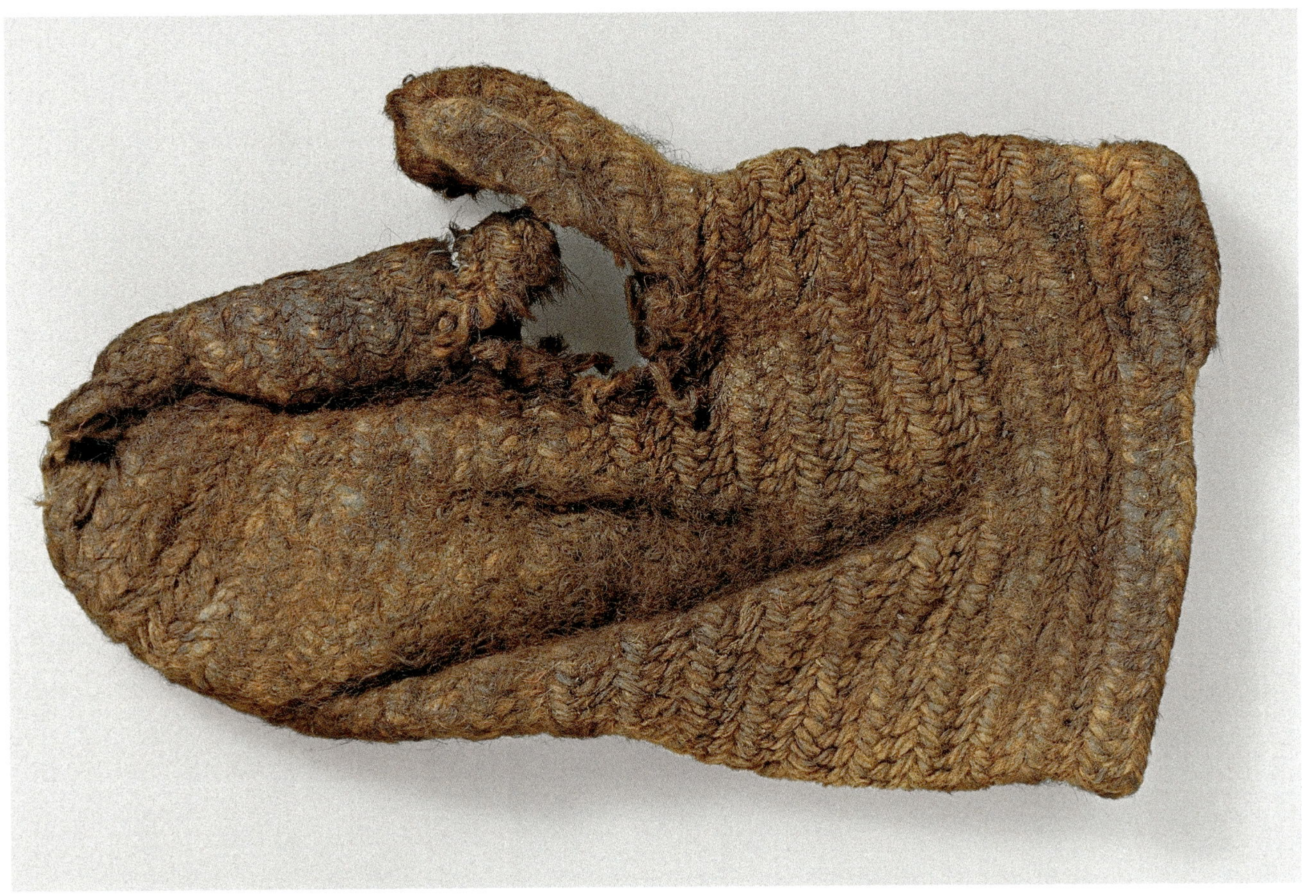

on being tensioned around the base of the thumbnail to achieve a consistent size, although it is also possible to tension them around a needle once you have had a little practise.

The stitches in this section belong to different 'families', and are often grouped using the name of a region, depending on whether they have two phases to their construction ('Finnish' stitches, to which Oslo and Mammen stitches belong), or three phases ('Russian' stitches, such as Dalby). These broad groupings can help the nalbinder find related stitches that build on familiar skills and can help clarify the many similar-looking stitches that rely on a subtle variant in working order.

Many of the thumb-tensioned stitches make attractive braids, and when you are practising stitches without a specific project in mind, you may find that the starting chains are useful as appliqué trims.

In this section we will look at these three thumb-tensioned stitches. If you are new to this style of working, I recommend that you try them in order.

Above: Eleventh-century mitten from Oslo, worked in either Oslo or Mammen stitch. Museum of Cultural History, University of Oslo, Norway/ Eirik Irgens Johnsen. Public Domain/ CC BY-SA 4.0

Oslo, Dalby and Mammen stitches compared

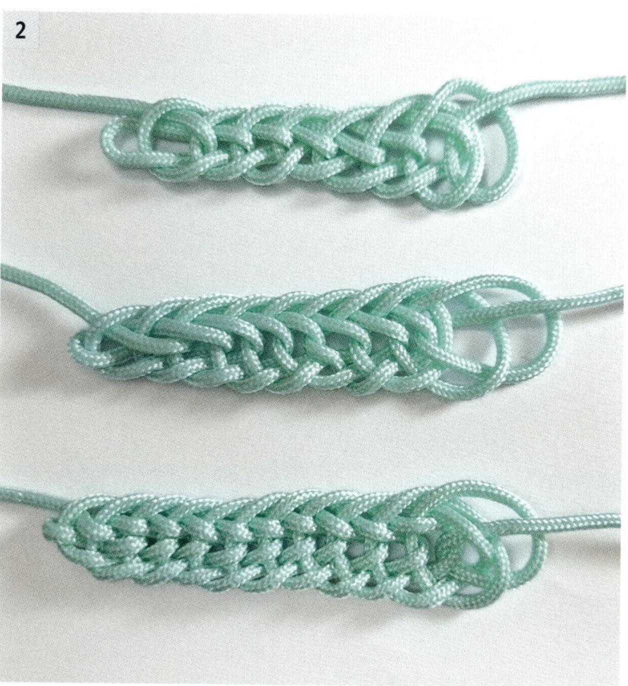

Two images of Oslo (upper), Mammen (middle) and Dalby (lower) stitches – image 1 shows the appearance of pulled-tight finished versions in wool; image 2 demonstrates the structure of these stitches prior to being tightened/compacted.

All three of the samples pictured in **A** were worked with the same number of stitches (25 stitches and five rounds) using the same yarn, the same needle and the same thumb. They are related stitches, but they clearly take up different amounts of space and have subtly different textures. Being able to work variations allows you to choose stitches that best suit the project you are planning.

Let's start by looking at the parts of a typical Oslo stitch as it appears on your thumb and the common abbreviations used when noting down a working order (**B** overleaf).

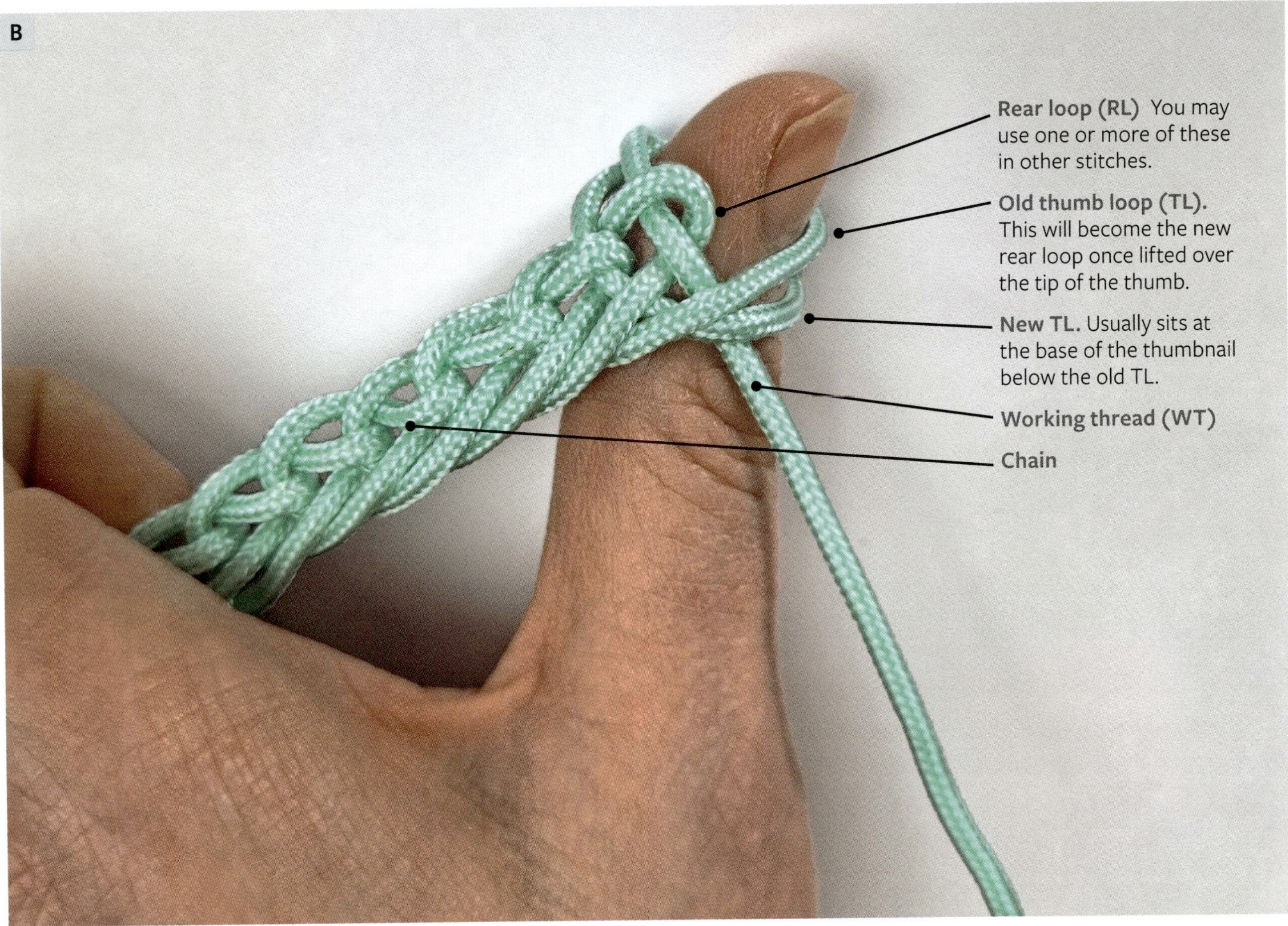

Tips for working thumb-tensioned stitches

- Take your time and aim for consistency. The biggest problem beginners face is keeping the loops the same size. This can be solved by making sure the stitches are formed around the same part of your thumb each time. For most people, the base of the nail is a good location.

- It is much easier to understand the stitches if you work through the instructions with yarn and needle in hand. Don't be afraid to rotate your hand so you can get a good look at how the loops sit from different angles as you get a feel for each stitch.

- If you have problems getting each new thumb loop to form where you want it, look at the direction in which you are pulling your yarn through. At first, it is often easiest to pull directly towards you over the V of the thumb and hand, but this can slant your new thumb loop in different directions, and as your confidence grows it is good to develop a habit of drawing the yarn through parallel to the base of your thumbnail.

- Give yourself permission to try each new stitch a few times and to mess it up initially! You learn far more by making mistakes and observing what went wrong than if it goes perfectly all at once.

- Many of these stitches will initially bunch up into something resembling a loopy caterpillar. You will need to gently stretch out and wriggle your starting chain to settle all the loops into place. You might be surprised how something that looks like a mess suddenly becomes even and much longer.

- These stitches lend themselves well to being fulled and can be good bases for embroidery. Yarns that full can most easily be joined by using a felted join, but if that isn't a good option for your yarn, try a Russian join (see Joining in new yarn, p. 26).

Oslo stitch

HANSEN'S NOTATION: UO/UOO F1

Oslo stitch is part of a family of nalbinding stitches traditionally tensioned on the thumb, lending themselves to lofty, warm and quickly worked-up projects. Oslo is one of the most popular stitches in contemporary nalbinding and is one that many people come across when seeing nalbinding for the first time. It is a good one to learn early on in your nalbinding journey, as several other thumb-tensioned stitches are easy to pick up once you can compare their working order to that of Oslo.

The Oslo-stitch projects include a simple hat worked from the base up, which is great as a first project and has a couple of options for shaping, and a spiral-worked hat in two colours worked at the same time from the top down.

The technical illustrations here are in a very smooth yarn for clarity, but many people prefer a lightly spun roving-style yarn for thumb-tensioned stitches. If you are using this type of yarn to learn Oslo, Mammen or Dalby stitches, and you find the fluffy nature of the yarn obscures your stitches, it might be a good idea to try a smoother plied yarn while you work out how the stitches are formed.

Working Oslo stitch

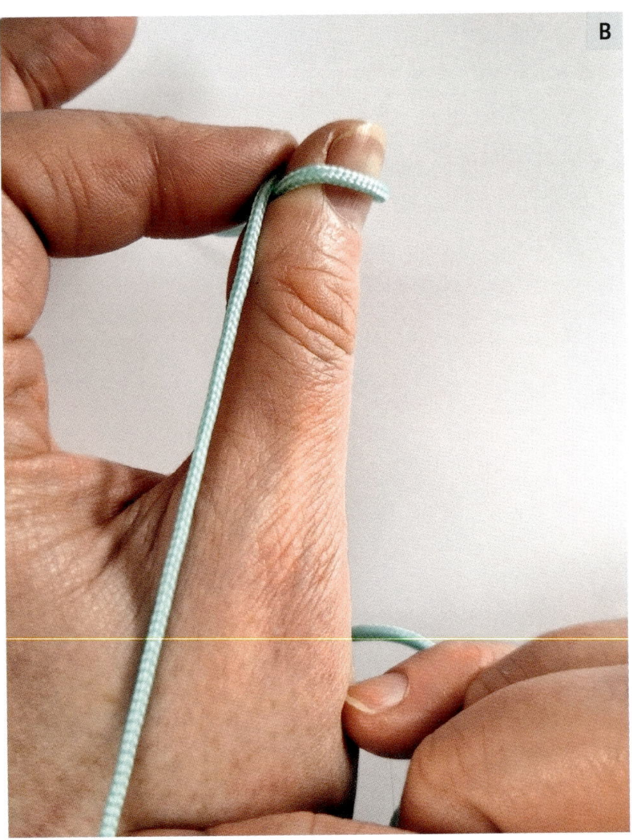

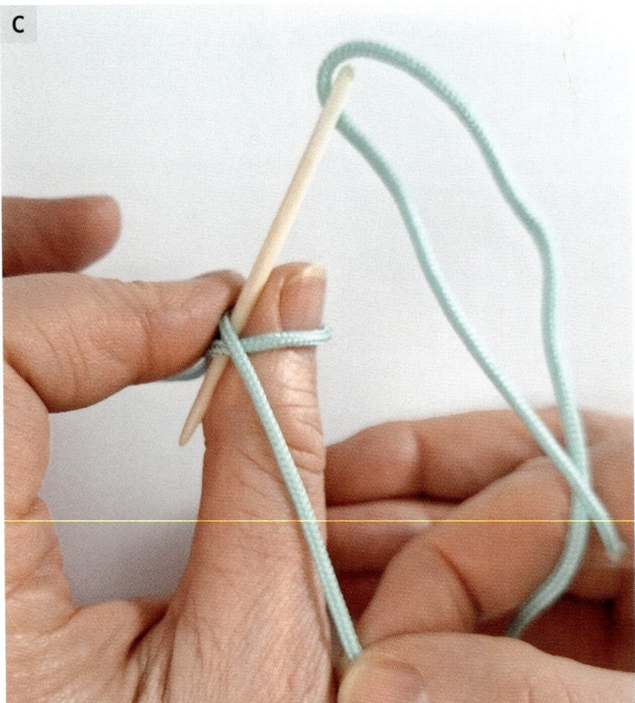

1. To set the stitch up, use a piece of yarn of one or two arms' length and either make a loose overhand knot in one end of it or wrap the yarn around your thumb (**A**) to form a loop.

2. Position this loop at the base of your thumbnail, so that you can lightly pinch the knot between your finger and thumb. The working end of the thread should be coming over the V between finger and thumb (**B**). This is your first thumb loop (TL).

3. Take the point of the needle and put it through the TL at the point where you are pinching it (**C**). This is often called the 'cross'. You will be going under both threads. The needle is pointing towards the V of your hand.

4. Pull the needle through over the V in your hand and you should see a second loop form. Watch that it doesn't jump off your thumb tip as you pull.

5. You want this to sit below the old TL, ideally around the base of your thumbnail (**D**).

6. These steps set up the two loops necessary for Oslo stitch. From here on you will use two main motions to form each stitch.

7. To make the stitch, use the point of the needle to gently push the old TL (nearest the tip of your thumb) off so it becomes a rear loop (RL). Leave the needle in place poking through the loop (**E**). You will put the needle tip through this point in Step 9.

8. Rotate the needle with the RL on it anticlockwise so that it goes over the edge of the RL (**F**) until you can insert it behind the cross where it is being pinched between thumb and index finger (**G**). Pull the yarn through to create the new TL below the old one.

9. Repeat these two motions until you have a chain of stitches. Don't worry if they look a little crumpled up at first (**H**), as once you have made a section of chain you can gently stretch it out to become much more even looking (**I**).

Working in the round from a chain start

This is the simplest way to start any project that has a section of tubular work, such as a mitten or hat.

1. Make a chain just a little longer than your desired object. This is because the second row will pull everything in slightly. If you feel your first couple of stitches are irregular, make the chain long enough to be able to unravel these starting loops later.

2. Bring the end round so that the first loop of your chain is adjacent to your current working stitch (**A**). Double check that it is not twisted! A deliberate twist can be very useful for a Moebius scarf, but usually isn't what you are aiming for.

3. Make your desired connection. Oslo can be worked either with an F1 or an F2 connection. This just means that you pick up the front loop (F1) or go through that and the loop that sits behind it (F2) when joining. Either is fine, but try to be consistent. In this example, I am using an F1 connection (**B**).

C

4. Make your stitch as normal. You don't need to do anything else to the loop that you have picked up (**C**).

5. Pick up the next loop to make a connection and take another stitch (**D**).

6. Work in the round until you need to shape your work. For simple projects such as bags where you intend to sew the base shut, wrist warmers or similar, you may be able to work solely with a tube.

7. At the end of your project, look at the start of your chain, and if there is a spare loop, gently unpick the end until you can tighten and sew in the tail neatly.

D

Increases and decreases

Increases are made by working twice into the same stitch. First pick up your connecting loop then work your stitch as usual. Then put the needle back through the same connecting loop and work another stitch. You now have 2 stitches where you originally had 1.

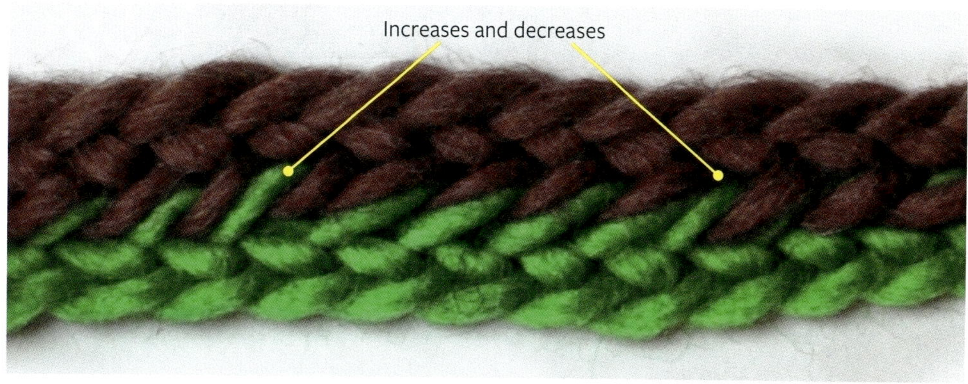

Decreases are made either by picking up two connecting loops at once, or by skipping a stitch before making the connection.

Round start

You may decide to start projects such as hats and mittens from a flat chain at the brim or cuff, decreasing as needed to close the crown or the finger cap. However, a round start in Oslo can be very useful, especially once you realise that starting with a different number of stitches will give completely different shapes, even if you then apply the same basic formula of increases.

Detailed instructions are given here for a round start of 12 stitches. This is generally a good starting point for thumb-tensioned stitches where you want the initial few rounds of work to lie in a flat circle. Later, you can compare it to a round start made with 8 stitches and to one made with 16 stitches to see what happens.

Abbreviations
Inc: work 2 stitches into each loop of the row below
Work x plain: work 1 stitch into each of the next x loops/stitches
Rep *-*: Repeat instructions between asterisks all the way around

1. Make a starting chain of 12 stitches (not counting the one active on your thumb) (**A**).

2. Thread the tail of yarn onto a needle and run it through the bases of those 12 stitches. You can do this from either end, and it's a good plan to experiment to find out which direction gives you the neatest start. Here I've worked from the same end as the working thread so the stitches sit on a ring of yarn (**B**).

4. Pull the tail to turn the braid into a round start (**C**).

5. You will be using an F1 connection, so put the needle tip through the next available front loop. This will join your new stitch to the row below (**D**).

6. Make your next stitch as usual. This is the first stitch of Round 1, where you will need to increase.
Round 1: Inc in each loop of the row below. 24 stitches (**E**).

Tips

- After you have worked a few stitches on Round 1, check the tail end of the yarn and if necessary, tighten the loop to keep the start neat.

- Although there is an optimum number of increases for a flat circle in each stitch type, nalbinding is very forgiving and if you find yourself a stitch out at the end of a round, or realise you accidentally put a stitch in the wrong place, don't worry – it usually all works out within a row or two.

Round 2: *Inc, work 1 plain*, rep *-* (**F**). Don't forget to gently wriggle your stitches at the end of the round to sort out any 'caterpillar' like bunching at the back.
Round 3: *Inc, work 2 plain*, rep *-*. 36 stitches. (**G**).

E

F

G

Tip – Reading your work:

- Look carefully at your work. It should be lying flat, and an imaginary line drawn across the working stitch will be at right angles to the circle. This tells you that the stitches are neither too crowded nor too sparse for a flat circle.

- If this line leans back towards your braid, another increase or two might be useful for a flat circle.

- If it is leaning forwards, or if the circle is developing a rippled edge, there are too many stitches for the circle, and you will need to work without increasing until it lies flat again.

- Being able to read your work like this will help you make increases and decreases more by intuition than by following a set pattern, making nalbinding extremely responsive to designing as you go.

Now let's work the same three rounds, but this time on a starting circle of 8 and 16 stitches respectively. See what happens. The 8 start becomes a gentle cone shape, very useful for sock toes or mitten tops, but the 16 quickly becomes crowded, and in this example, I stopped at the end of Round 2, because it's already clear that it has too many stitches.

In most cases, every additional increase row will have one more plain stitch between the increases. Decreases are done in reverse; for example, let us imagine you have just worked 7 plain; you will then work 2 stitches together for a decrease. The next round will be 6 plain, then a decrease. The third round will be 5 plain, decrease, and so on.

Decreasing into a flat or curved top from a tubular piece of work uses the same logic. Work 2 stitches together, followed by several plain. Put plain rounds between decrease rows for a curved top.

Some projects don't need any shaping at all. The Moebius scarf project makes the most of the tendency of a starting chain to twist, creating a flat-looking project that is still worked in the round. You can do this in almost any stitch, but Oslo is an excellent choice and really gives you a chance to focus on practising the stitch while still creating something wearable.

Above & below: Starting in the round using 8 stitches (left), 12 stitches (middle) and 16 stitches (right)

PROJECT 9

PROJECT 9
Moebius scarf

Short scarves can be worn close to the neck (and make good hairbands). Alternatively, make it long and wide for a draped accessory that looks fabulous over a winter coat or sweater. This is a great use for yarn that has variegated shades within it. If you have just one precious skein of hand-painted yarn in mind for this but aren't sure if it will be enough, consider using that first; if the scarf isn't wide enough, add a border in a plain contrasting shade to each side to frame the feature yarn. In this sample, I used one skein of variegated yarn and then switched to dark blue to create a solid edge.

Above: The sample pictured here shows the starting tail of the yarn in purple before it was woven in during finishing. The twist means that your scarf will grow out from a central point, and if using stripes of colour, these will appear on both edges of the scarf at the same time.

DIFFICULTY: Simple

RECOMMENDED STITCH: Oslo

JOINING METHOD: Felted or Russian

You will need:

- Approximately 100g yarn/100m (328ft), or more for a wider scarf

- A needle

1. Make a chain a little longer than the intended length of the scarf. Take your time when joining the chain into a round – it is important to introduce one twist to the chain.

2. Work plain until the scarf is as wide as you want it! That's it.

3. Finish off ends neatly. Rinse your work gently and pat it into shape on a towel to dry.

PROJECT 10
Oslo-stitch hat

This simple hat begins as a chain and is worked in rounds until it is time to decrease for the top. At this point, you can either follow the basic principles for decreasing a circle or decrease intuitively to give pointy tops. The three hats here start the same, but use different decrease rates to give varied tops. This project is for a classic round-topped hat.

DIFFICULTY: Simple
JOINING METHOD: Simple, Felted or Russian

You will need:

- Approximately 55g/55m (180) of bulky yarn. Choose something in which you can see the stitches

- A needle

- A stitch marker to help keep track of decreases

Abbreviations

Dec: work 2 stitches together
Work x plain: work 1 stitch into each of the next x loops/stitches
Rep *-*: Repeat instructions between asterisks all the way around

1. Make a starting chain slightly longer than the head size needed (**A**). Most thumb-tensioned stitches pull in a little as you get to the second row, so a little extra room is a good idea. My sample used 72 stitches.

2. Join into a round, checking that the chain is not twisted (**B**). I've left a starting loop to be unpicked later for a neat finish.

3. For the body, work rounds of plain Oslo stitch until the hat is deep enough at the sides. Try it on regularly. Although most hats just need plain stitches until the desired height is reached, it is better to put in occasional increases or decreases when necessary, rather than let it get too far along at not quite the right size. Expect to work somewhere between 8 and 10 rounds in most cases (**C**).

4. For the crown

Round 1: *dec, work 4 plain*, rep
-. 60 stitches. (*See* **C**).

Round 2: Work plain. This gives a
gentle curve to the start of the
decreases.

Round 3: *dec, work 3 plain*, rep
-. 48 stitches.

Round 4: *dec, work 2 plain*, rep
-. 36 stitches.

Round 5: *dec, work 1 stitch plain*,
rep *-*. 24 stitches.

Round 6: *dec*, rep *-*. 12 stitches.

A slight difference in the number of
stitches remaining won't matter.

Alternatively, for a pointed top
work the first few decrease rounds
as above, but then additional plain
rounds between each decrease
round to create a point as tall as you
wish. You can do this just in the last
2 or 3 rounds for a neat little 'stalk'
on top of the hat as shown here (**D**)
or start earlier for a more gradually
pointed top. Experiment!

5. When you are down to around 12 stitches (or
fewer if doing a pointy top) tighten your final
stitch, draw the thread through the remaining
loops and weave in the ends (**E**).

6. To finish, check the hat is a good length,
then undo any surplus loops at the start of
the chain and weave in the ends. Then lightly
dampen it and arrange to dry (**F**). If your hat
is just a bit too big, you can full it slightly if
the yarn will shrink, and block it while damp
over something the right size (or wear it
while it dries a little) to get the perfect shape.
Alternatively, try something like an applied
braid or a little embroidery at the edge to pull
it into a better size. It may also make a good
gift for someone with a larger head!

Troubleshooting

If, after getting part way through your hat, you try it on and decide it's a little bit tight, you can always work downwards from the starting point later, adding a few stitches in the next round to make it slightly bigger. You may wish to carefully unravel a few loops to get to a point where you can see what is going on enough to start working downwards. This is also a good tactic if the hat turns out to be a little too short after finishing the crown.

Spiral stripes hat

A basic hat shape can look much more interesting worked in two shades. A clever spiral start lets you work alternating colours evenly, and a top-down construction based on the round start we looked at earlier gives a neat smooth crown. I have used a roving-style aran-weight yarn for the sample.

DIFFICULTY: Intermediate

JOINING METHOD: Felted or Russian

You will need:

- Approximately 55g/55m (180ft) bulky yarn in 2 shades

- 2 needles (optional – you can use the same needle on whichever shade you are working with)

- 2 stitch marker

1. Start by making 2 chains of 6 stitches each (not including the current working loops on your thumb). Take your time and make them as neat and even as you can. This will help get a clear starting spiral. If useful, make an extra stitch, then undo the starting loop.

2. Lay these facing each other so that the tails of yarn are at the top and bottom respectively (**A**).

3. Thread the tail of each starting chain through the bottom of the stitches of the other (**B**). You will go through 6 stitches, with the remaining ones being the current working TL.

4. Pull up the tails and the 2 chains will close into a round start. You should have 12 stitches plus the 2 active ends. Your next stitch at each end will pick up a connection from the other colour (**C**).

D

E

Round 4: Work plain. This is to start introducing a slight curve to the crown of the hat. Have a good look at your work after this round. If the disc is still lying completely flat or if it has any waviness at all to the edge, work another plain round before moving on to Round 5. You should be starting to see a curve after this round.

Round 5: *Inc, work 3 plain*, rep *-*(**F**). 60 stitches.

Round 6: Work plain. If your hat is wide enough continue to work plain, but be ready to add more increases if you feel a little more width will suit your intended head better.

Round 7: If you feel you need another complete increase round, work *Inc, work 4 plain*, rep *-*. 72 stitches.

7. For the body, work in circles, alternating colours so that the stripes spiral around each other. Try it on occasionally! When your hat is as large as you want it to be, you can decide whether to finish the different shades on opposite sides of the hat or work one a little further to bring the final stitches to the same side. Make the final stitches smaller to allow a neat finish.

F

5. Place stitch markers at the points where the colours change. From here on the increases are worked one half round in one shade, then one half round in the second.

6. For the crown:
    Round 1: Inc in each stitch around. 24 stitches (**D**).
    Round 2: *Inc, work 1 plain*, rep *-*. 36 stitches.
    Round 3: *Inc, work 2 plain*, rep *-*. 48 stitches (**E**).

8. To finish, weave in ends, and lightly dampen and shape the hat before leaving to dry (**G**).

   If you used an F1 connection, the inside of the hat will show a slightly different stripe pattern to the outside (**H**). You can use whichever you prefer as the right side.

Variations: You can work this with 3 colours as well! Set up your starting circle with 3 sections of 4 stitches each instead of 2 sections of 6.

Hot-water bottle cover

This cosy and useful project uses just a little shaping and is finished with a simple ribbon closure at the base to allow you to secure the bottle. Try something that works up fast like Oslo stitch for this. The thickness of nalbinding is perfect for insulating the bottle.

DIFFICULTY: Simple

RECOMMENDED STITCH: Oslo

JOINING METHOD: Felted, or Russian if your yarn won't felt

You will need:

- A soft, bulky yarn. I used around 100g/100m (328ft) of roving-style yarn

- A needle

1. Begin at the bottom with a chain slightly longer than the circumference of the bottle.

2. Work in the round until you reach the shoulders and mark each side with stitch markers (**A**).

3. For the shoulders and neck:
   Round 1: *Dec, work plain to the marker, dec*, rep *-* once more.

   Repeat Round 1 another 3 or 4 times until you reach the neck of the bottle, then work in the round until the neck is covered.

4. Weave in the tail neatly. The top is left open to allow the bottle to be filled without having to remove it from its case.
   You could full this slightly if desired. Thread a ribbon through the loops along the base and tie the case shut to enclose the bottle.

Mittens

Many pairs of nalbound mittens have survived the centuries, and they are still useful projects today. Nalbinding lends itself well to garments that take a lot of wear, and because it is harder to unravel than knitting it takes longer to wear out a pair of nalbound mittens than their knit equivalent. We will look at a very simple pair of fingerless mittens within the section on Mammen stitch, but in this project, we will look at the anatomy of a more structured mitten with a gauntlet cuff.

Whether you work cuff up, or fingers down, as with socks, I recommend that you work both mittens at once. In most instances, they are made identically so they work on either hand. If you are working with very specific yarn shading you might want to think in terms of right and left mittens, but that is an artistic decision rather than a technical one.

The tactics for shaping socks work here too. Start cuff-up mittens with a chain big enough to pass your hand through easily and continue in rounds until the cuff is long enough. Add a few stitches to allow for the size change as the hand approaches the thumb.

Start finger-down mittens with a round start and increase to create a cup shape that covers the top of the fingers. Work in rounds until it is time to begin the thumb. Begin with more stitches than you would for socks or a hat: this means that there is extra thickness at the tips of the fingers, which is where you need it in a pair of mittens.

The easiest way to add a thumb is to work the bulk of the mitten first, just like the Mammen stitch handwarmer project later in this chapter, leaving a slit where the thumb is to go. When the rest is finished, go back and add the thumb.

Troubleshooting

It is common to find small gaps where the thumb joins the hand of the mitten. These can usually be tightened by gently adjusting the tension of the stitches on either side, but it is OK to darn a scrap of yarn across these areas on the wrong side if you can't tighten! If you are going to full the mittens, any small adjustments like this will blend in and become almost invisible.

Gauntlet mittens

Classic cosy mittens with a long gauntlet wrist, fulled for extra warmth, with optional fringing. If you don't live somewhere that requires heavy mittens, these make fabulous oven gloves! I used a bulky roving-style yarn for the sample, and plied yarn for the fringe, as it will mat together less in the fulling stage giving you more control over the final finish.

DIFFICULTY: Intermediate
RECOMMENDED STITCH: This sample recipe is worked in Oslo, but many stitches are possible
JOINING METHOD: Felted or Russian

You will need:

- Approximately 150g/150m (492ft) warm, lofty yarn
- A small amount of plied yarn, if adding fringing
- A needle

Abbreviations

Dec: work 2 stitches together
Inc: work 2 stitches into the next loop/stitch
Inc 2: work 3 stitches into the next loop/stitch
Work x plain: work 1 stitch into each of the next x loops/stitches
Rep *-*: Repeat instructions between asterisks all the way around

A

This mitten is worked from the cuff up and is sized for a large adult hand. It will initially look huge but will full into something extremely dense and warm.

1. Start with a chain of 44 stitches and make a round ready to continue work.

2. For the cuff:
   Rounds 1–3: Work plain.
   Round 4: Dec 3 times as evenly as possible around the cuff. 41 stitches.
   Round 5–7: Work plain.
   Round 8: Repeat Round 4. 38 stitches.
   Rounds 9–10: Work plain. Use stitch markers to mark the start and middle of your round, where you will make some increases where the thumb widens out from the wrist.

Tip:
Wherever possible, centre your increases on the stitch markers, but don't worry too much if they are slightly to one side or the other. The forgiving nature of nalbinding means this will even out in the fulling stage.

Round 11: Inc into each of the next 3 loops, work plain to end of the round. 41 stitches.
Round 12: Inc 2 into each of the next 3 loops, work plain to the next marker, inc into the stitch after the marker, work plain to end of the round. 48 stitches.
Round 13: Work plain (**A**).

3. For the thumb slit:
   Round 14: Work plain until there are 6 stitches left before the last marker. Make a chain of 4 new stitches, count 6 stitches past the marker into the next round and reattach the work to the seventh stitch (**B**). You have skipped 12 stitches. This difference in stitches makes the shaping for the narrower part of the hand. You now have 40 stitches.

4. For the hand:
   Rounds 15–21: Work plain.
   Rounds 22–23: Dec 10 times as evenly as possible around. 20 stitches.
   Round 24: Pull the remaining 20 stitches up into a closed circle and weave in the ends.

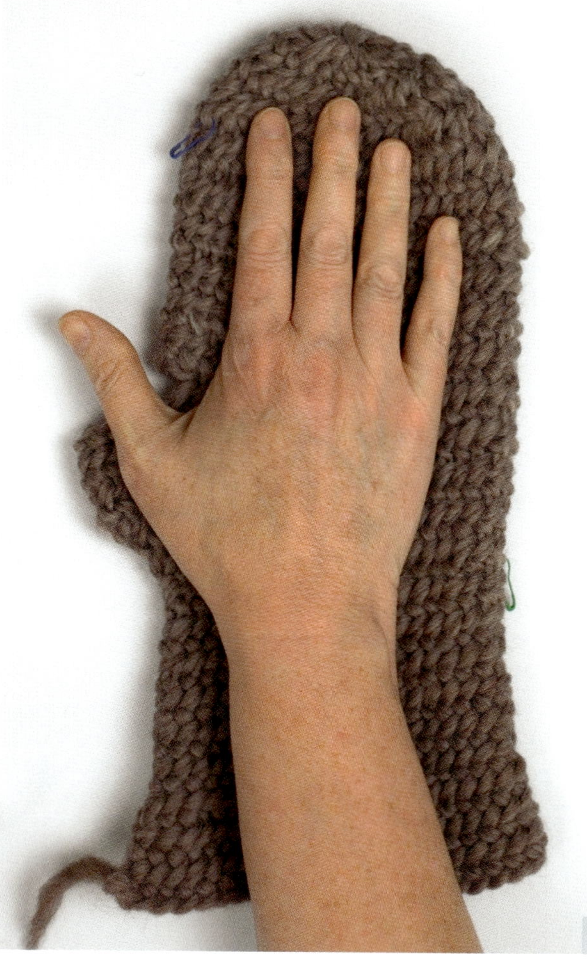

This denser closing circle makes for thick fabric where your fingertips need it most in the mitten (**C**). It should look far too big (**D**)!

5. For the thumb, you will be working into the thumb slit. It can be useful to make one set-up stitch on your thumb before starting to pick up the stitches. This can be unpicked and the end darned in later if necessary.

   Round 1: Reattach your yarn and work into each loop to give 16 stitches. If you appear to have too many stitches, work 2 loops together at the corners as necessary; this helps to avoid gaps.

   Rounds 2–5: Work plain.

   Round 6: Dec by picking up 2 loops onto the needle each time. 8 stitches.

   Round 7: Dec as in Round 6 until you can close the top of the thumb with a stitch (**E**).

E

6. To finish, weave in the ends, paying attention to the join between thumb and hand where any small gaps can be darned in. Check whether you prefer the inside or outside of the mitten. Sometimes the inside surface gives a neater finish in which case turn them inside out (**F**).

7. Full the mittens until they are approaching the right size. This sample was fulled most of the way to their final size, then a fringe added to the bottom edge (**G**) before one final light fulling. You may find a crochet hook useful for adding the fringe, although fringing can also be looped in using a needle (**H**).

   Putting the fringe in after the first fulling lets you avoid matting the fringe into a confused lump, while still achieving the felted effect on the final strands. Don't be surprised if the mittens change shape while fulling; its normal for nalbinding to get longer when wet, and it can take a fair bit of rubbing and kneading to shrink the work back to the final size. It will get there though.

   When fulling mittens, you can do a lot of the work by putting them through the washing machine on a very gentle cycle but do be aware that it is very easy

F

G

H

to overdo the shrinking this way and end up with something too small. For a safer way to full and for the very best shape do your final fulling (if not all of it) by hand while wearing the mittens.

Put them on and wash your hands thoroughly in hot soapy water. This settles the final shape exactly to your hands. Blot your mittens while still wearing them using a towel, then very carefully ease them off and allow to dry. Be careful not to stretch them out of shape when removing them.

Mammen stitch

HANSEN'S NOTATION: **UOO/UUOO F2**

This stitch is essentially Oslo stitch with one more loop picked up. This makes the work thicker and denser, and you will find the same number of stitches make for a smaller finished object. It is usually worked with an F2 connection. When an F1 connection is used, this stitch tends to be called Korgen stitch.

Working Mammen stitch

1. To set up, wrap the yarn around your thumb to form a loop (**A**). Pinch this point between finger and thumb throughout the stitch.

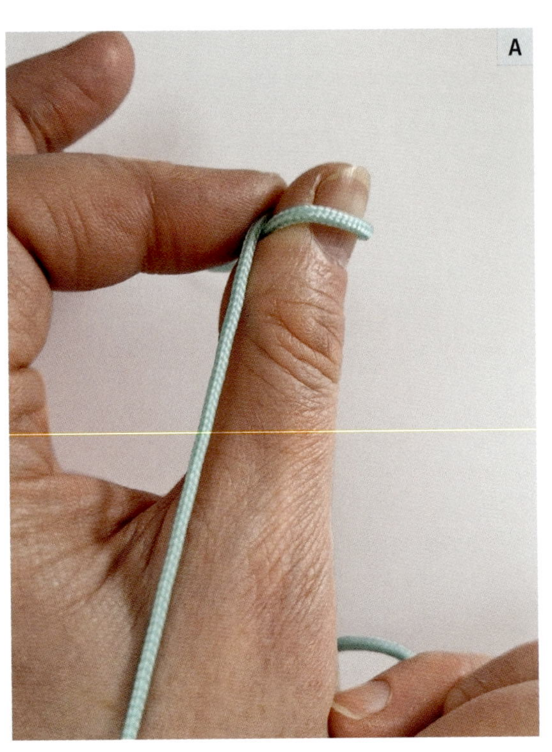

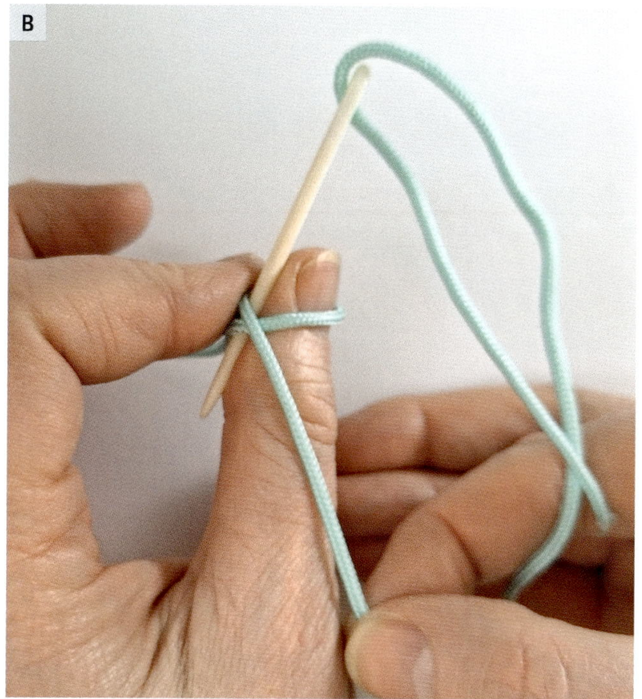

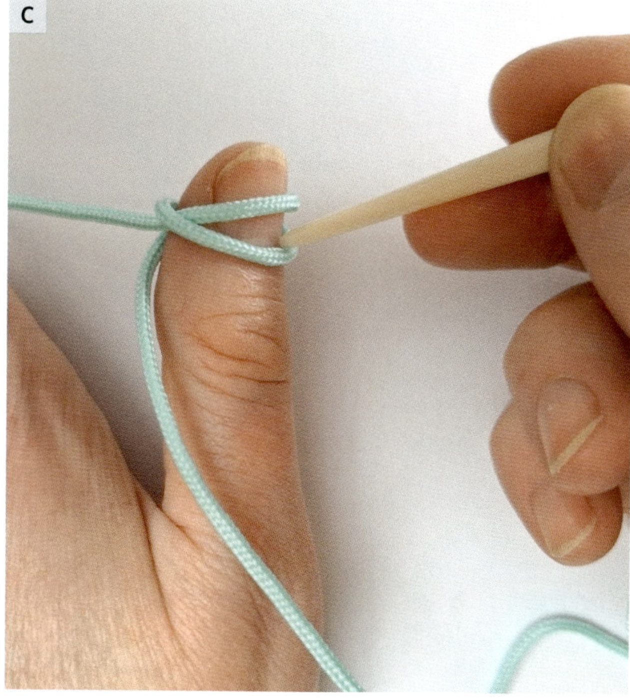

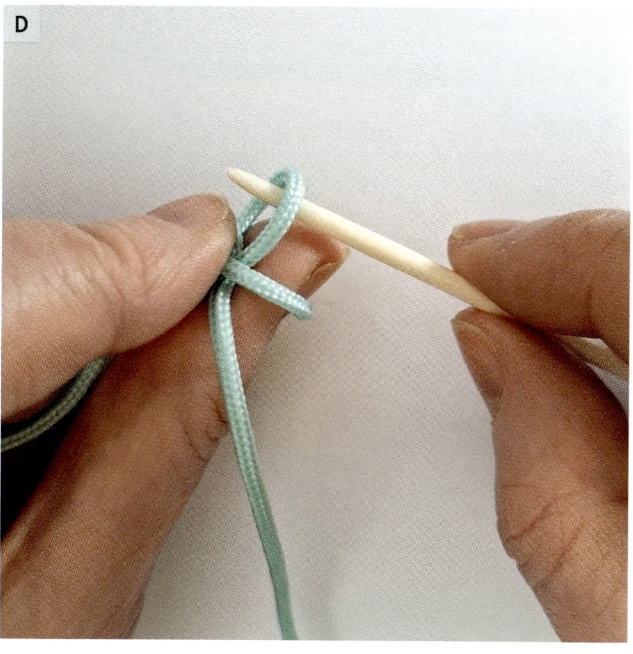

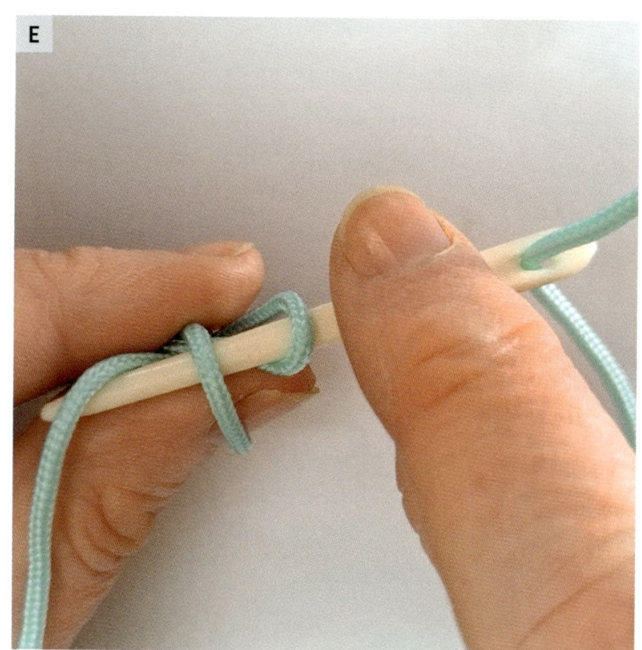

2. Put the needle tip behind the cross made between the TL and WT (**B**).

3. Pull through towards you to form a new TL below the old one (**C**).

4. Slip the top TL off to form a RL, keeping the needle tip through it (**D**).

5. Rotate the needle tip anticlockwise until you can put it under the cross and pull through (**E**).

6. Slip the top TL off to form a RL (this is step one of the next part).

7. Now inspect the back of your thumb. You should see two rear loops (**F**). Mammen stitch differs from Oslo stitch in that you will put the needle tip through both RLs before going through the cross.

8. To make the stitch, slip the top TL off to become a RL, keeping the needle tip in it, then go through the old RL as well (**G**).

9. Rotate the needle anticlockwise to put the needle tip under the cross and pull through to create a new TL below the old one (**H**).

10. Repeat Steps 7 and 8 to create your starting chain (I).

11. Once some chain is made, gently stretch it out to remove any bunching up of stitches (J).

Fingerless mittens

These simple and extremely cosy handwarmers are a good way to get a feel for working Mammen stitch, and require no increasing or decreasing unless you wish to add extra shaping. Creating a thumb slit can make space for an afterthought heel or thumb to be added later when working more complex socks and mittens.

DIFFICULTY: Simple

JOINING METHOD: Simple, Felted or Russian

You will need:

- Approximately 65g/65m (213ft) of a bulky roving-style yarn

- A large needle

- If your yarn is limited, it's a good plan to make both mittens at once; that way if you run out of yarn you can decide whether to make them shorter or to switch to a different colour to finish off.

1. Make a starting chain long enough to go round the widest part of your hand (**A**). Mine used 32 stitches.

2. Join into a round, and using an F2 connection, work until you reach the lower joint of the thumb (**B**). This may take around 8 rounds. You could opt to add a couple of increases to accommodate the base of the thumb at about Round 6, but as nalbinding makes a stretchy fabric this generally isn't necessary. This sample was worked with no shaping.

3. The thumb slit will take up roughly a quarter of the circumference, so divide your number of stitches by 4 (8 in this case) and make a chain of that many stitches (**C**).

4. Count 9 or 10 stitches along your work and reattach the chain (**D**). The hand is narrower above this point and a slightly smaller tube makes for a neater fit around the palm.

5. Continue to work in rounds until your mitten is long enough. This will usually be somewhere between the base of the fingers and the first knuckle.

6. To finish, make the final stitch smaller by adjusting the tension off the thumb, then weave in ends.

Dalby stitch

HANSEN'S NOTATION: **UOU/OUOO F1**

In more recent centuries, we see nalbinding used in detailed folk-art forms. Dalby mittens and Sorunda mittens are typically embroidered styles found in Sweden. Dalby stitch is associated with these and lends itself well to items fulled after working. When closely examined, it became clear that not all these beautiful 'Dalby mittens' were made using Dalby stitch. Yet again, this is an example of a region having a range of working styles and several available, similar-looking stitches.

We will use the mittens shown overleaf as inspiration for the application of additional ornamentation to nalbound items, using simple embroidery techniques

to create attractive modern accessories. These fit in well to a lifestyle that values comfort and practicality and celebrates the time spent on embellishment of functional objects.

Dalby stitch can appear complicated at first, but if you have become comfortable with Oslo stitch, there are just a couple of additional steps. That said, it is very important to pay attention to the direction in which your needle points at each step.

This stitch has the benefit of lying very flat with a regular surface, and the stitch itself is deep, so items made using it are moderately fast to work. It is well suited to bags and cases where stitches that curl are less aesthetically pleasing.

Above: **Mid twentieth-century Dalby mittens.** Collection of the author

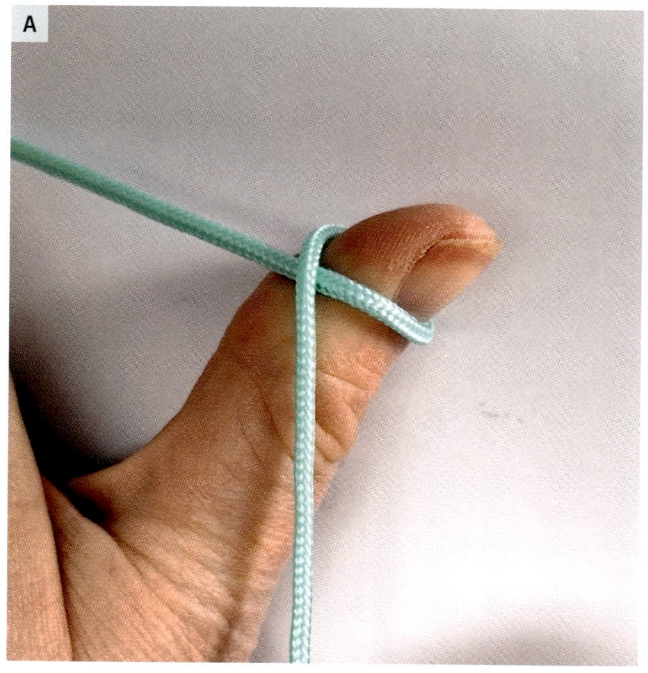

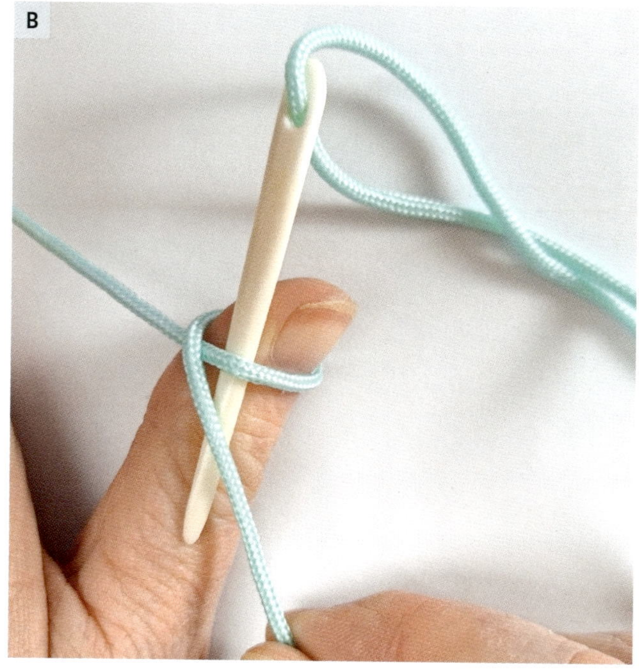

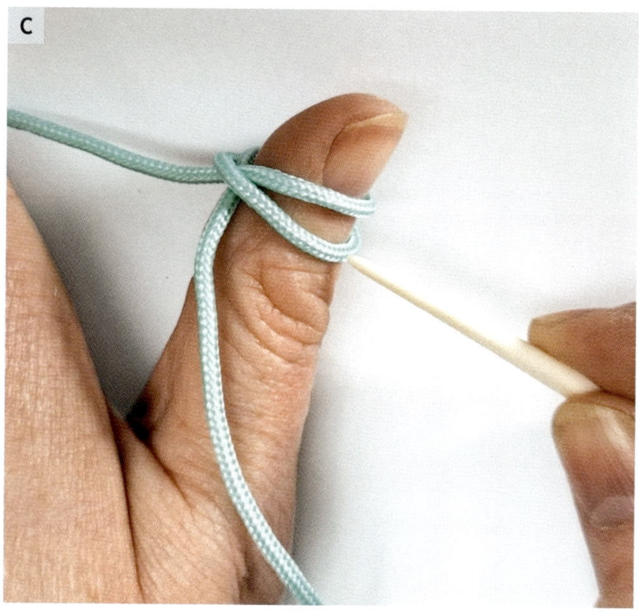

Working Dalby stitch

1. To set up the stitch, create the first loop by wrapping the yarn around your thumb with the working thread (WT) coming towards you. Pinch the cross over between finger and thumb; it is shown more open here for clarity (**A**).

2. Put the needle behind the cross in the yarn and pull through to create a new thumb loop (TL) (**B**).

3. This new loop (pointed to by the needle) should sit below the old TL at the base of your thumbnail (**C**).

4. Lift the old TL off the tip of your thumb so it becomes the first rear loop (RL) (**D**).

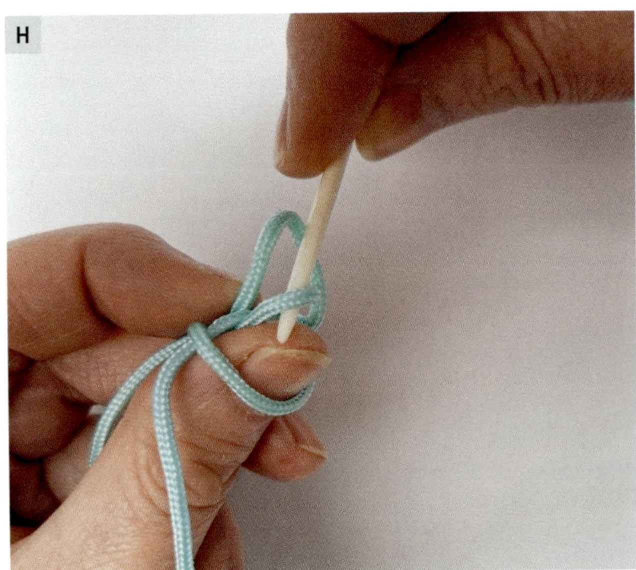

5. Poke the tip of the needle through the RL then rotate it anticlockwise until you can put it under the cross formed by the TL and WT (**E**). Pull through and you should once more have two thumb loops. To this stage it is just like starting Oslo stitch.

6. Pick up the old TL with the tip of your needle (**F**) and carry it over the first RL so that it sits just behind it (**G**).

7. Put the needle tip through the RL working from back to front (as if you were aiming to poke your thumb with the needle) (**H**).

8. Now rotate the needle clockwise, with the loop on it, until up you can pick up the old TL that you moved a moment ago. You should notice that the 2 loops sit in a little cross on your needle (**I**).

9. Turn the needle anticlockwise until you can put the needle under the TL and the WT (**J**).

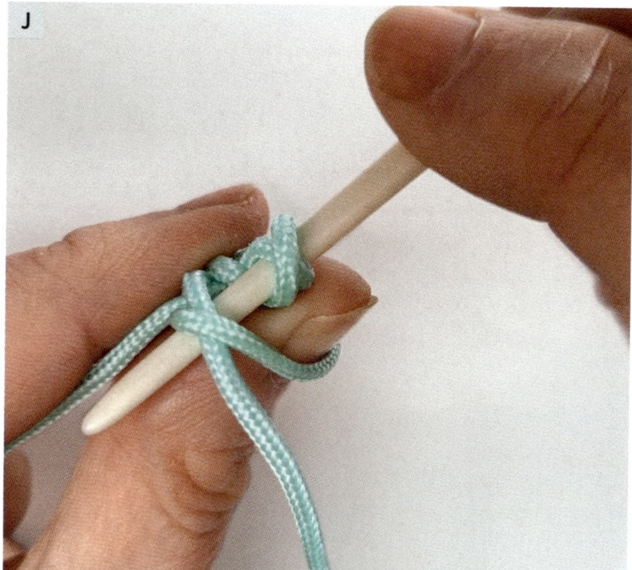

10. Pull the yarn through, and you should have 2 loops on the thumb again, the new one nearest the base of your nail and the old one just above it.

   To make the stitch there are now 3 main steps:

11. Move the old TL over the current RL.

12. Rotate the needle towards you (anticlockwise) to pick up the RL from the back, then rotate away from you (clockwise) to go through the old TL. This makes a crossed stitch.

13. Rotate the needle towards you to go under the TL and under the WT, then pull the yarn through to make a new TL.

14. Once the starting chain is underway, you'll see that it forms a regular, even braid (K) and that the RL sits quite neatly at the back of your thumb – pointed to here by the needle (L). You may occasionally have to locate it with the tip of your needle before starting the next stitch.

15. Joining to a preceding row is generally done as an F1 connection.

PROJECT 15

Tablet or journal case

This project draws inspiration from the beautifully embroidered Dalby mittens, but in a simplified form that makes it ideal as a first exploration of this stitch. The same project could be worked in any stitch that doesn't curl too much at the edges.

You will be fulling (felting) your finished project, so it may be a good idea to work a small sample first and see how much it shrinks. If in doubt, aim to make it about 20 per cent wider than your intended object. Dalby stitch will shrink more in width than in height when fulled. You will need to choose a yarn that will felt for this project.

DIFFICULTY: Intermediate
JOINING METHOD: Felted or Russian

You will need:

- Approximately 40g (for the smaller case) or 80g (for the larger case) of aran-weight yarn that will felt

- A needle

- Embroidery threads

- A suitable needle for the decoration

- Optional: a button and closing loop

1. Make a starting chain about 20 per cent longer than the circumference of the object that will go in the case (**A**). If you find your first stitches are uneven, it is a good idea to unpick them until you have a chain that is smooth on which to base the rest of the project.

2. When your chain is long enough, bend it round towards your working hand in a C shape to allow you to start picking up connecting stitches to form a second row (**B**).

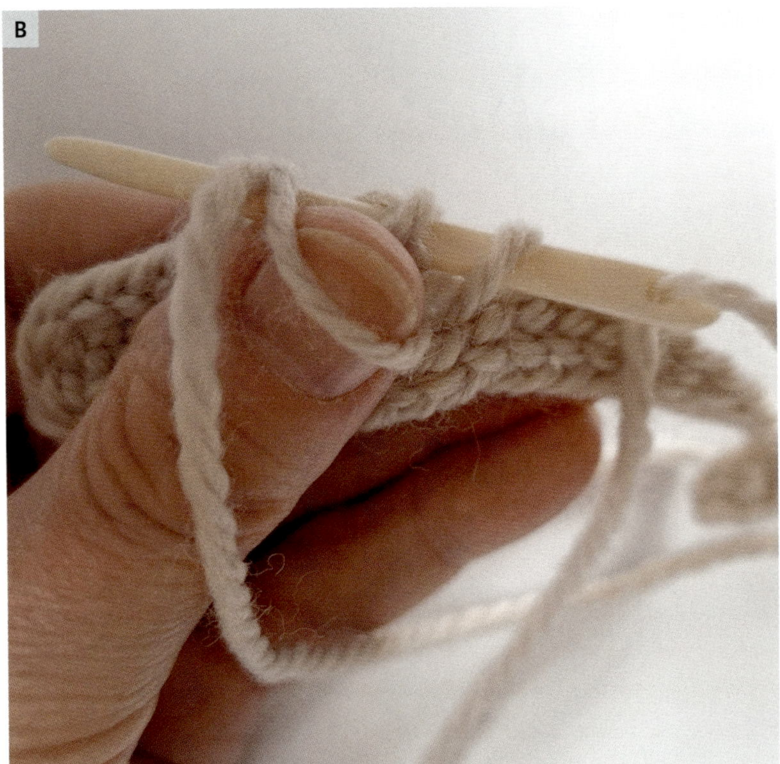

3. At the end of this row, continue round the end of the chain to pick up the other side, so you now have a long, slim oval shape. This is the base of your case. In this instance we don't need to add any increases as the slight contraction that forms as you go around the end of your starting chain makes a neatly curved seamless base to your case (**C**).

4. Work around in circles until the case is slightly larger than the intended object. Weave in the ends neatly. Because Dalby stitch is deep, you may wish to tension the last couple of stitches on the needle rather than on the thumb to allow a smooth transition to finishing off.

Fulling your work

For this sample I've started with an approximately square bag before fulling (**D**).

Softly spun yarns usually felt quite easily, and you may find you have more control fulling by hand than in the washing machine. Both methods are given; choose whichever you are most confident with. The idea is to firm and shrink the work but not to completely lose the stitch definition. Dalby stitch tends to shrink more in width than in height when fulled.

If you are fulling by hand, fill a sink with hand-hot, soapy water. Start by washing the bag gently and don't be surprised if it gets slightly bigger at first as the yarn softens and stretches. Keep washing and rubbing it between your hands, gradually becoming more vigorous, until it begins to shrink. Roll it up and rub it some more, then roll in the other direction. Keep going until it is the desired size. Rinse thoroughly, blot dry in a towel and shape carefully before allowing to dry.

If using a washing machine, put the bag in on a very gentle short cycle with something else, like a few t-shirts. Many machines have a 15-minute quick wash for delicate garments, which would be an ideal start. When it finishes, get the bag out and give it a good wriggle to avoid uneven fulling or creasing and to stretch it to the required dimensions. Expect to put the bag through two or three wash cycles to get to the required size. Shape carefully and allow to dry.

My sample here has changed very little in length but has become narrower as the fulling has drawn in the stitches (**E**).

Decorating your bag

A plain bag has its place, but this lovely fulled surface is perfect for a little embroidery. If you are new to this, use simple stitches and don't be too ambitious. Our sample here is inspired by the Dalby mittens but doesn't pretend to achieve the detail seen on the originals. A few flowers or some swirly vines and maybe an initial or two will all look good. If you spotted any small errors in your stitches, a strategically placed flower can easily cover that up.

The nalbound fabric base is thick, so you probably won't find an embroidery frame any help. Take your time and make sure you don't pull the base out of shape while stitching.

The key to successful embroidery on surfaces like this is to keep it simple. Try basic crewel-work stitches and, while cotton embroidery floss can be used, wool embroidery yarn will give a feel that is more true to the

style of embroidered nalbinding that inspires this project.

Sketch your intended design on paper if it helps you visualise it, then work each element in a logical order.

Stem stitch is ideal for laying out the stalks of the flowers (**F**). Work it like an upside down backstitch.

Lazy Daisy stitches make great small flowers such as for-get-me-nots. The same stitch can also make simple small leaves. Work as follows:

1. Bring your yarn up through the fabric, then down into the same place to form a loop (**G**).

2. Without pulling it tight, bring the needle up where you want the top of the petal to sit and catch the loop on the thread (**H**).

3. Go back into the same place to make a tiny stitch that holds the loop open. For flowers, take the needle back to the centre point to begin the next petal (**I**). Repeat for the desired number of petals. 5 is usually a good option.

French knots (bullion stitches) are ideal for making the centres of small flowers. Work as follows:

1. Bring the needle up to create a large loop of yarn (**J**).

2. Wrap the needle 3 or 4 times with the yarn end that comes out of the project before pulling the needle through (**K**).

3. Stitch back into the fabric to secure the wrapped thread into a small knot.

4. Satin stitch makes dense petals for carnations, pansies, and other larger flowers and leaves (**L**). Overlap shades for added depth (**M**).

5. Finish edges with a brightly coloured blanket stitch if desired (**N**). This is a touch often seen on the original mittens, as is a simple crochet edging.

Knotwork capelet

Having learnt three variations on thumb-tensioned stitches, it can be a lot of fun to combine two of them into one project so that you can really see how they lend themselves to different uses.

A straightforward shoulder capelet can be made very dramatic looking with an interlaced braided border. This is much simpler than it sounds, especially if you start with the braid then work up! Choose a yarn with decent stitch definition for the braid, but don't be afraid to use something different for the capelet itself. I used bulky roving-style yarn for the sample.

DIFFICULTY: Intermediate. Most of this is very simple, but it is a larger project and can use two different stitches.

RECOMMENDED STITCHES: Dalby for the braid, Oslo for the capelet

JOINING METHOD: Felted or Russian

You will need:

- Approximately 150g bulky roving-style yarn
- A needle

1. Set up 3 chains approximately long enough to wrap around your shoulders. Keep the working loops available to add more.

2. Start braiding them together (**A**) and make them longer as necessary until the braid fits loosely around the part of your shoulders that you want as the bottom edge of the capelet.

3. Join the ends together neatly (**B**). You can hide each join behind one of the overlapping braid sections if you wriggle each end along slightly.

4. Check the braid is arranged evenly. It may help to put a few pins in to hold everything steady for the next part.

5. For the body, start a chain to be the base of the rest of the capelet. This could be in the same stitch as the braid, or you could move on to a different stitch if desired. As it passes an upper loop on the braid, make connection stitches into the upper two or three loops, then if needed a plain stitch to take you to the top of the next loop of braid. In this sample 3 connecting loops are made then straight on to the next braid loop (**C**). My sample had around 112 stitches after joining the braid to the body of the capelet (**D**). Once the braid is attached all the way around, double check nothing is twisted, then carry on in the round until it is time to shape the shoulders.

6. For the shoulders, decrease gently for 2 rounds. I worked as follows:

> **Round 1:** *Dec, work 11 plain*, rep *-*.
> **Round 2:** *Dec, work 10 plain*, rep *-*.

Don't worry if your stitches don't precisely divide into the decreases; near enough will work just fine.

Now decrease a little more rapidly to reduce the head opening size.

> **Round 3:** *Dec, work 5 plain*, rep *-*.
> **Round 4:** *Dec, work 4 plain*, rep *-*.

7. Try it over your head before deciding about the next round. For a scoop neck this may be a good place to stop. My version has a funnel neck, so I decreased a little bit more until the neck was snug but I could still pull it over my head.

8. Work a few rounds if desired for the neck, then taper off the last stitch or two (**E**).

9. To finish, weave in any ends, rinse through gently and pat to shape before leaving to dry.

PART FOUR: SOCKS, TECHNICAL INFORMATION, REFERENCES

Socks and slippers

Many of the projects suggested in this book can be worked in more than one stitch, allowing the user to experiment with, and develop, their repertoire and skills. A particular feature of nalbinding is that it does not need detailed patterns in the same way as knitting or crochet. Patterns are more a series of guidelines about shaping, structure and fit that can be applied to any stitch and yarn gauge as the project grows.

Nalbinding has traditionally been used for socks, and there are so many ways to approach the heel that it's worth looking at these all together. There are several sock projects within the specific stitch sections of this book, but let us look more generally at how to structure and shape socks.

Stitches

Socks have been made using many types of nalbinding stitches. York stitch, cross-knit looping, Oslo, Mammen and Dalby are all good choices, as are many others that we have not explored in this book.

Working two at a time

If possible, work both socks at once, using one length of yarn on one, then the same on the other. This means that you are always at the same stage on each sock and any changes to the recipe can be applied to both straight away. It also means that if you are using hand-spun, painted or remnants of yarn you will have enough for each area of the sock.

Sizing

Feet are often a funny shape. Arches may be high or flat, toe profiles may have different shapes and ankles may be slender or robust. Fortunately, nalbinding is stretchy and the ability to make slight changes as you go along makes socks very adaptable.

I recommend that you make your first socks in a size that will fit you so that you can try them on regularly and adjust as you go. A table of typical sock lengths is given here to help make it easier if making for someone who is not available for trying things on. Remember that there is only a 'barleycorn' of length between shoe sizes (this is roughly a third of an inch) and because socks stretch, any given pair will fit a few different sizes.

Sock size	UK shoe size	EU shoe size	US shoe size	Overall sock length, heel to toe (cm)	Overall sock length, heel to toe (in, to 1/4 inch)
XS	1–2	34–35	2–3	23	9
S	3–5	36–38	4–6	24.5	9 ¾
M	6–7	39–41	7–8	26	10
L	8–10	42–44	9–11	27.5	10 ½
XL	10.5–12	45–47	11.5–13	29	11 ¼
XXL	13–14	48–49	14–15	30.5	12

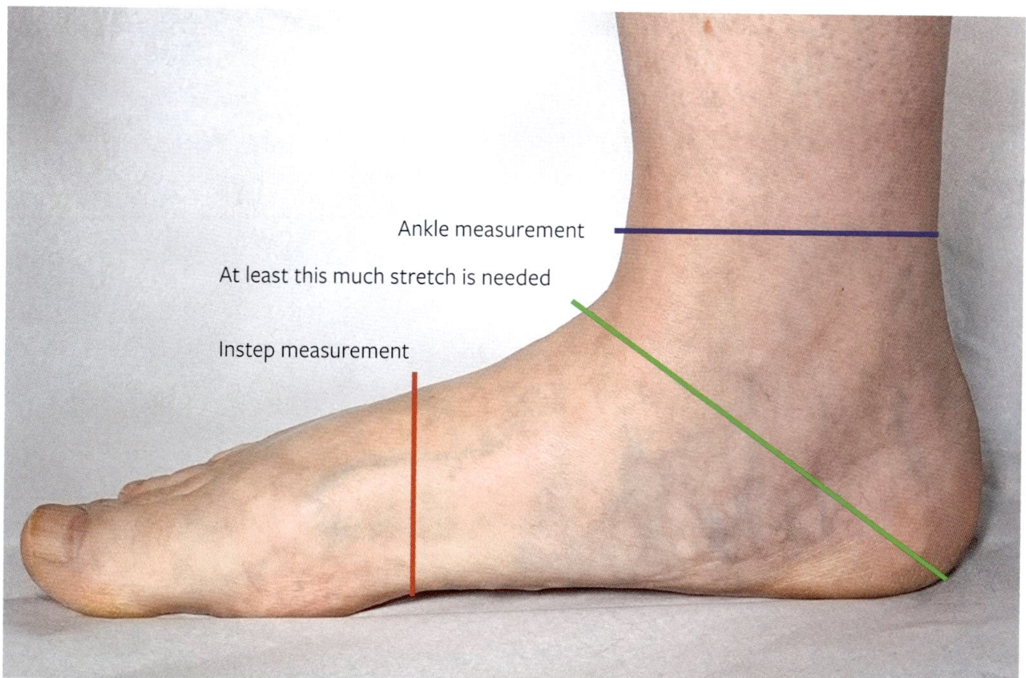

Left: Feet are variable, but many people don't have the same measurement at ankle as they have at instep, and you need extra room to get the sock on and off

Nalbinding tends to stretch more lengthways than widthways, especially when being pulled on and off a foot or hand. This means that you may need to slightly adjust your design to appear a little wider and shorter than seems necessary when you are working it.

Fit around the ankle

Depending on whether you are working toe up or cuff down will affect whether you need to make many adjustments to this area.

Look at the image of the foot above and compare the lines which show the difference in size between the foot at the top of the arch, diagonally across the heel, and round the ankle. Different feet will also have different proportions. Your best tactic is to keep trying on the sock and adjust as you go while you gain practise at estimating fit.

First, decide whether you want to work from the toe to the cuff, or from the cuff to the toe.

For cuff down, start with a chain slightly wider than the intended ankle or calf. Most nalbinding stitches pull in slightly once the second round goes in. Work in rounds until you reach the top of the instep then go on to the heel section.

For toe up, begin with a round start that is suitable for your chosen stitch. You want the toe cup to curve almost immediately, so you can use fewer stitches than you would have done for a flat circle. Work a toe cup that completely covers the toe joints. Work in rounds until you reach the top of the instep, adding increases as needed, then go on to the heel section.

Heels

There are many ways to shape a sock heel, and this section includes instructions for some of the most frequently used methods. Once you are familiar with these, you may find you can develop variants that work well for your particular preferred yarns, working style and desired fit.

PROJECT 17

Short-row heels

Have a look at a pair of typical modern socks. They are highly likely to have a short-row heel. This method works the same way for cuff down socks as it does for toe up.

DIFFICULTY: Intermediate
RECOMMENDED STITCH: Oslo
JOINING METHOD: Felted or Russian

You will need:

- Approximately 80g/120m (393ft) plied aran weight yarn for this ladies UK size 6 sample pair.

- A needle

A

1. Make the toe and instep section, or the cuff if working down, as you did with project socks in earlier chapters (**A**).

2. To begin the heel, work flat on roughly half the stitches that you have available in successively shorter rows until the back of the heel is reached (**B**). To do this, turn your work to continue the next row flat, but without making any provision for an extra stitch as you turn. This will automatically make each row shorter as the 2 loops of the stitch currently on your thumb become the turn, and as you pick up the next available loop the row will become 2 stitches shorter.

3. When you reach the back of the heel, work back at right angles to the narrowed section (**C**).

> **Row 1:** Pick up the end of the row below and increase into the first stitch, work plain to the end of the row, increase into the last stitch.

Repeat Row 1 until you get back to your original number of stitches.

4. You should now be able to work in rounds to finish the rest of the sock (**D**).

Troubleshooting:
It can take a little practise to pick up the second half of the heel without leaving small holes, but if this does happen, you can weave a scrap of yarn along this line from the inside, catching in any loops that did not connect. This will settle in unobtrusively, especially if the sock is to be fulled (**E**).

PROJECT 18
Flap heels

DIFFICULTY: Intermediate
RECOMMENDED STITCH: Cross knit looping
JOINING METHOD: Felted or Russian

You will need:

- Approximately 130g/185m (607ft) plied aran weight yarn for the adult pair pictured.

- A needle

Variants on this technique are seen quite often on Romano-Egyptian children's socks (see Project: festival socks, p. 69).

1. Work the toe and foot until you reach the instep, then work flat on sufficient stitches to make a good sole section, aiming to keep the rows the same length each time until the back of the heel is reached. You can choose to work a couple of short rows here for a smoother turn, but it works fine left square.

2. Work backwards and forwards around the outside of this square flap, rejoining to the sock as you reach the sides until you are high enough to either work a split ankle or start going round in circles again.

Tongue heels

This method is a little different in that you start the shaping as soon as the toe cup just reaches the knuckles of the toes rather than waiting until the instep is reached. Lewins (2004) reports that this is a traditional Scandinavian method.

Because this is an all-in-one method, you will create a complete sock. This sample used a roving-style yarn in Oslo stitch, which makes a good base for a felted slipper.

DIFFICULTY: Intermediate
JOINING METHOD: Felted or Russian

You will need:

- Approximately 95g/95m (312ft) roving style yarn for this pair.

- A needle

Abbreviations

Dec: work 2 stitches together
Inc: work 2 stitches into the next loop/stitch
Work x plain: work 1 stitch into each of the next x loops/stitches
Rep *-*: Repeat instructions between asterisks all the way around

1. The toe cup shown was started on 8 stitches.

   Round 1: Inc into each stitch around. 16 stitches.

   Round 2: *Inc, work 1 plain*, rep *-*. 24 stitches.

   Round 3: *Work plain.

2. For the sole, work a length of chain that reaches almost to the back of the heel, then turn this and work back along it to rejoin the toe cup (**A**). The chain shown was 20 stitches long.

3. Work around in circles. A lighter shade is used here for clarity.

   Round 1: Increase into each of the 5 stitches at the back of the tongue at the heel point and decrease 3 stitches together at the corners (see arrows, **B**). This will create a flat sole while the toe cup continues to get longer.

   Round 2: Increase 7 times at the heel, and decrease 3 together as the work turns to go round the toe cup (**C**).

4. Try it on to check whether the back of the heel has been reached and, if necessary, work further rounds. This sample was long enough, so I stopped increasing at the back of the heel but continued to decrease at the corners where the toe cup joins to form the ankle area.

5. For the foot section, shown in dark purple, I decreased 3 stitches together at each corner until it was the right size (**D**). With this project, the aim was to felt the sock into a slipper shape, so I stopped before shaping the ankle section. If you would like to work the slipper further up the ankle, continue to work plain with no further decreases. The sock may look a little unstructured off the foot, but this shaping gives a remarkably comfortable fit when worn.

6. Lightly full the sock if a slipper is desired. I used a shoe last to give a good shape (**E**), but you can wear the freshly fulled slippers while damp and allow them to dry on your feet for a while for a similar result.

D

E

Squashy socks

This project is a reliable way to work your first pair of socks with an afterthought heel. Essentially, you will work until the heel area is reached, then make a chain that goes around the ankle (or instep, if working cuff down). Continue to work in rounds until the sock is done, then go back and pick up stitches for the heel.

DIFFICULTY: Simple

RECOMMENDED STITCH: This sample recipe is worked in Oslo, but many stitches are possible.

JOINING METHOD: Felted or Russian

You will need:

- Approximately 80g/120m (394m) of plied sock yarn – this is usually harder wearing than the very lightly twisted roving-style yarn often favoured for hats, mittens and scarves.

- A needle

1. Start at the toe with a round start of 8 stitches.

2. Work a cup shape until it covers the base of the toes. Mine ended up at 36 stitches (**A**).

3. Work in the round, adding occasional increases if necessary, until the top of the instep is reached (**B**). My sock had 38 stitches and another 10 rounds by this point.

4. For the ankle, make a chain long enough to go around the back of the ankle and reattach on the other side by passing the needle through 2 loops. It will be roughly half the number of stitches as the instep around, but adjust to fit the foot as needed (**C**). From here you can work around the top edge of the ankle; you may find it easiest to reverse the direction to suit.

5. Paying particular attention to the points where the chain rejoined at the ankle to minimise holes (although these can be resolved later), work in the round until the ankle is high enough (**D**). In my sample, I could have done a better job at reducing the holes at the join by adding an extra stitch to the chain then working 2 stitches together on the next round at this point to close the gap.

6. For the heel, the first round picks up the stitches in the hole left in the work. From here on you need to reduce at the corners where the instep joins the ankle. The exact number of stitches may vary with yarn, tension and stitch, but try reducing 3 stitches into 1 on each side for about 3 rounds and see how you get on.

7. In the last round or 2, decrease then work 1 plain and repeat all the way around to narrow the gap faster.

8. Run the end of the yarn through the remaining few stitches and draw the hole closed.

9. If there are any small gaps where the ankle joins the cuff and heel, darn these in with matching yarn. Wash through to allow the yarn to bloom and settle in the stitches. This method also lends itself well to light fulling after finishing.

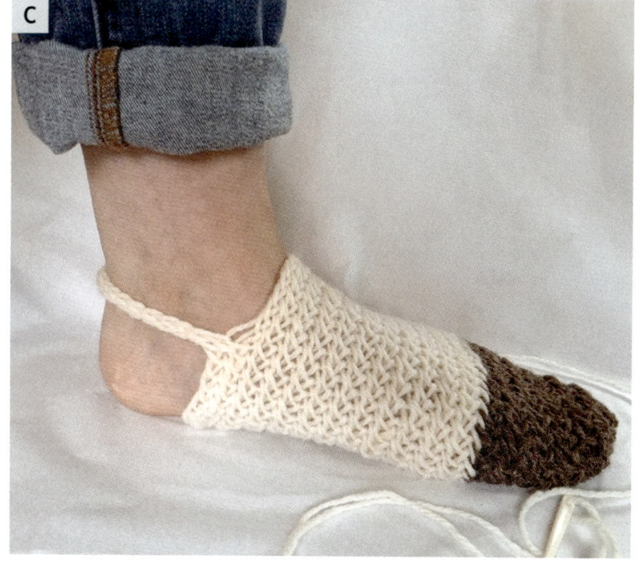

Getting technical: Nalbinding notations

Nalbinding is a highly intuitive craft that requires little in the way of formal patterns, and there are potentially thousands of ways to create stitches, with several dozen in regular use today. Despite, or perhaps because of this, there have over the years been attempts to produce notation systems to describe the structure of different nalbinding stitches.

It is not the intention of this book to go into nalbinding notation in detail, so I will use just a couple of examples to outline the principles. If you have a mathematical mind you may wish to explore stitch notation further: there are stitch dictionaries that list a dazzling number of variations, all of which can be deciphered once you can visualise the path the yarn takes. It is perfectly possible to learn and use many stitches without ever needing to refer to notations, so if they are not the way your brain works, please don't worry about it!

Hansen's notation (Hansen 1990) is probably the most frequently encountered system, sometimes incorporating variants suggested by more recent researchers. Toini-Inkeri Kaukonen's system, developed in 1960, grouped stitches commonly used in Finland into 'families'. Notation systems were also developed by Nordland and Hald to help them describe stitches found in their research (Nordland 1960; Hald 1980).

Kaukonen's notation does not cover all stitches, but is still very useful as a way of describing stitches according to whether the needle passes under or over different numbers of groups of threads. These are referred to as 'phases', although they do not specifically reflect the number of motions that the needle makes. Kaukonen classified nalbinding stitches based on how many yarns the needle crosses before the direction of the needle changes in the middle of the stitch. For example, Oslo is Finnish Stitch 1+1, Mammen is Finnish Stitch 1+2, and Dalby is Russian Stitch 1+1+1.

Hansen's notation system describes the path of the yarn within the stitch as a series of Unders (U) or Overs (O), with the turn indicated by a forward slash (/). The notation may also list what type of connection is most usually used. This is why a stitch such as York can be described as UU/OOO F2, while Dalby stitch is UOU/OUOO F1.

Hansen's descriptions are most useful for beginners to check that the stitch you have made really is the one you were aiming for. Take a section of nalbinding and lay it flat so the loops are clearly visible, then trace the path from where the yarn enters the stitch. For a right-handed worker, the path will be clockwise.

Look at these two samples. **A** shows Oslo stitch, and **B**, Mammen stitch, which differs from Oslo only in going through two rear loops instead of one. Laid flat and annotated, the unders and overs can be systematically traced.

The same stitches in Kaukonen's notations are described by the number of loops that remain around

the thumb, and the number of stitches that get picked up behind the thumb by the needle. Hence Oslo is Finnish 1 +1, because one loop remains on the thumb, and one stitch is on the needle as it turns to go under the cross and make the new stitch. Mammen is Finnish 1+2, because it starts very like Oslo, with one loop remaining on the thumb, but two loops are picked up by the needle before it turns to make the stitch.

Above: Oslo Stitch, UO/UOO and Mammen stitch, UOO/UUOO with Hansen's notations overlaid. Read the notation from the bottom right, finishing where the yarn leaves the stitch.

Conclusion

Nalbinding is a craft with vast possibilities. Although we have explored some of the most frequently met stitches and project types, there are potentially thousands more ways to pass a needle and yarn through a series of loops, and there are dozens of named stitches currently in use.

The same stitch may appear very different when worked in plant fibres and a tight needle tensioned gauge, compared to the same stitch in a lofty yarn and tensioned to the thumb. Fulling the work further increases the possibilities for creating structural forms, and it can be combined with other crafts such as embroidery or crochet to give unique results.

Take a moment to consider the uses to which our earlier ancestors may have put these loop manipulated stitches, and how we find similarities as well as regional variations around the globe. These insights can help inspire current craft projects and also remind us of the amazing skills and ingenuity of past generations. By sharing these skills we ensure that knowledge developed over thousands of years is not lost in our fast-paced modern world.

I very much hope that you have enjoyed this exploration of nalbinding and have found it a rewarding addition to your crafting repertoire. I'd like to wish you the very best of luck in your crafting journey, wherever it may take you.

Sally

Above: A practise sock can make a good place to store a collection of nalbinding needles

Right: On a fine day it is nice to sit outside and do some relaxing nalbinding in the sunshine. And if you're really lucky, sometimes you end up with a helper!

Acknowledgements

Project testers: Sophie Allan and Suzie Roberts valiantly tried out my early written descriptions and suggested many useful improvements.

As always, a huge thank you to my very patient family and friends, with particular thanks to Betty Pointer and Ashley Bennett.

A special mention to all the people who have attended workshops with me over the years. Craft techniques are often subjective, with more than one approach being possible. The methods shown in this book are the ones you have helped me determine as being ones that worked for the majority of you. Thank you all.

Left: Workshop participants show off their first explorations of different stitches

References

Andersen, S.H. (2013). *Tybrind Vig: submerged Mesolithic settlements in Denmark.* Jutland Archaeological Society, Hojbjerg.

Barber, E. J. W. (1991). *Prehistoric Textiles: The Development of Cloth in the Neolithic and Bronze Ages with Special Reference to the Aegean.* Princeton University Press, Princeton, New Jersey, p. 12 and p. 130.

Classen-Büttner, U. (2015) *Nalbinding – What in the World Is That? History and Technique of an Almost Forgotten Handicraft.* Books on Demand, Norderstedt.

Davidson, D. S. (1933). 'Australian netting and basketry techniques' in *The Journal of the Polynesian Society,42*(4), pp. 257–299.

Davidson, D. S. (1935). 'Knotless netting in America and Oceania' in *American Anthropologist,37*(1), pp. 117–134.

Decker, A .M. (2024). 'NOW: Kinzembe, Nkutu, or Zamba kya mfumu – Kongalese Prestige Cape 1962.1.14' in *Nalbound.* Available at: https://nalbound.com/2024/02/13/now-kinzembe-nkutu-or-zamba-kya-mfumu-congalese-prestige-cape-1962-1-14/ [Accessed 24 Aug. 2024].

Hald, M. (1980). *Ancient Danish textiles from bogs and burials. A comparative study of costume and Iron Age textiles.* Translated from the Danish by Jean Olsen. National Museum of Denmark, Copenhagen.

Hansen, E. H. (1990). 'Nålebinding: definition and description' in P. Walton & J. P. Wild (eds.), *Textiles in Northern Archaeology. NESAT III: Textile symposium in York 6–9 May 1987,* pp. 21–27. Archetype Publications, London.

Jacks-Svantesson E. (2011). *Vinterblomster: Nålbundna vantar från Dalby i Värmland.* Algusta.

Kaukonen, T.-I. (1960). 'Kinnasompelun levinneisyys ja työtavat Suomessa' in *Suomen museo LXVII,* pp. 44–73.

Lewins, S. (2004). *Nalbinding Socks: Methods of Construction.* Available at https://www.shelaghlewins.com/reenactment/naalbinding/sock_construction.htm [Accessed 2 Aug.2024].

MacKenzie, M. A. (2019).*Androgynous objects: string bags and gender in central New Guinea.* Routledge, Abingdon; New York.

Marian, C. (2008). 'Archaeological arguments concerning the textile technologies of Cucuteni civilization: nalbinding technique' in *Etablissements et Habitations Prehistoriques. Structure, Organisation, Symbole,2007,* pp. 327–34.

Nordland, O. (1961). *Primitive Scandinavian Textiles in Knotless Netting.* Oslo University Press, Oslo.

Otto, A. R. (2024). *Stitchcollection Needlebinding.* Independently Published, Amazon.

Schick, T. (1988). Nahal Hemur Cave. Cordage, basketry and fabrics. *'Atiqot'* (English Series), 18, pp. 31–43.

Soukup, M. (2023). 'Bilum and Noken: String bags and sorcery in New Guinea' in *Kulturní studia,21*(2), pp. 139–160.

Vajanto, K. (2014). 'Nålbinding in prehistoric burials: Reinterpreting Finnish 11th–14th-century AD Textile Fragments' In *Sounds Like Theory. XII Nordic Theoretical Archaeology Group Meeting in Oulu,* Vol. 25, No. 28.4, p. 2012.

Walton Rogers, P. (1989). *Textiles, Cordage and Raw Fibre from 16–22 Coppergate.* Archaeology of York, The Small Finds, 17/5. London, Council for British Archaeology.

Winiger, J. (1981). *Feldmeilen Vorderfeld: Der Übergang von der Pfyner zur Horgener Kultur.* Verlag Huber, Basel.

Yale.edu. (2024).*Knit Textile Fragment | Yale University Art Gallery.* [online] Available at: https://artgallery.yale.edu/collections/objects/5962 [Accessed 30 Aug. 2024].

Resources

There are many internet resources, and these can change with time, but at the time of writing these are just a few recommended sites for those wanting to explore more. These websites represent useful information and in some cases video tutorials of stitches.

Nalbinding playlist on my YouTube channel
www.youtube.com/playlist?list=PL5zgizOgAtq3Wdb7_mwuHcWEtwASs_lpa
Or search for Sally Pointer on YouTube. My videos tend to focus on early forms of nalbinding as part of a wider exploration of traditional skills.

Nålbinding: Facebook Group
www.facebook.com/groups/644499622267562
This active and friendly group is supportive of beginners and showcases modern and experimental work by inventive and inspiring craftspeople.

Nalbound: Exploring the history of the nalbinding technique
www.nalbound.com/author/sigridkitty
Anne Marie Decker's site has a valuable archive of historical items with a commentary on their structure and relevance, including a Nalbound Object of the Week. An excellent starting point if the global nature of nalbinding interests you.

Sanna-Mari Pihlajapiha
www.en.neulakintaat.fi
This site is particularly valuable if you are trying to understand the technical differences between nalbinding families of stitches, an aspect that we only briefly touched upon in this book. With a strong Finnish perspective, she largely follows Kaukonen's notations and often combines stitch descriptions and pictures with video links, making this site an extremely useful stitch dictionary.

Karin Byom
www.youtube.com/user/kbyom
https://www.instagram.com/karin_byom
Karin Byom is an experienced nalbinder who hosts a stitch of the month as well as occasional craft-along projects. Her account is useful if you'd like to explore other stitches and gain ideas for future projects.

Index